H. A. IRONSIDE
Ordained of the Lord

TITLES BY THE AUTHOR

Henry (Harry) Allan Ironside, 1876—1951
His Last Portrait, taken in 1949

H. A. IRONSIDE
Ordained of the Lord

E. Schuyler English

LOIZEAUX BROTHERS
Neptune, New Jersey

FIRST EDITION, JULY 1976
FIRST PAPERBACK EDITION, JUNE 1983

H. A. IRONSIDE: ORDAINED OF THE LORD
is a revised and expanded
edition of the 1946 volume
by the same author

Library of Congress Cataloging in Publication Data

English, Eugene Schuyler, 1899-
 Ordained of the Lord, H. A. Ironside.

 Revision of the ed. published in 1946 under title:
H. A. Ironside, ordained of the Lord.
 "The complete writings of H. A. Ironside": Pp. 239-242
 Includes index.
 1. Ironside, Henry Allan, 1876-1951. I. Title.
BV3785.168E5 1976 269'.2'0924 [B] 76-13873
ISBN 0-87213-143-2

Printed in the United States of America

To

ANN HIGHTOWER IRONSIDE

who helped a servant of God

finish his course

this book is affectionately dedicated

CONTENTS

PART 1

BOYHOOD DAYS

1

Henry Allan (Harry) Ironside is born, October 14, 1876—
Paternal ancestry—John Williams Ironside—Sophia Stafford—A second son—An early death.

2

A nineteenth century Dorcas—A lover of hospitality—
God's provision—An earnest soul winner—"Save my boy
early"—Religious though unconverted—Reading the Bible
through—An atmosphere of eternity.

PART 3

AMONG THE BRETHREN

PART 4

THE MOODY CHURCH YEARS

14

15

16

17

HAI's commentary on Isaiah—Cataracts removed, September 1950—Six beautiful, happy days—Showing off a little— Accident in Vancouver—Voyage to New Zealand—Reunion with the Laidlaws—Harry hospitalized with a heart attack—"I have just read seven chapters"—Harry called Home, January 15, 1951.

ILLUSTRATIONS

18 *Illustrations*

PREFACE

The year 1976 is noteworthy in evangelical circles because it marks the one hundredth birthday of the subject of this biography and also the centennial of Loizeaux Brothers, Inc., its publisher.

The Loizeauxs wanted to commemorate their own anniversary in a special way. The best-selling author of the firm's history is Harry Ironside, a fact that stands even though he has been gone for a quarter century. A new generation of readers has come along that knows his books but not their author. What better way to celebrate the double centennial event, the publishers asked themselves, than to tell again the life story of H. A. Ironside and his ministry? So they invited me to undertake the writing, not only, I suppose, because I wrote the earlier biography but also because I knew Harry Ironside well and was a part of some of his experiences during the last fifteen years of his life.

This volume is much more than a revision of H. A. IRONSIDE, ORDAINED OF THE LORD. The 1946 biography, which takes him to 1943, has been condensed and almost completely rewritten. The record of the years between that and 1951, when Ironside was called into God's presence, is entirely fresh and contains some highly interesting incidents of his later years.

It has been rewarding to review the remarkable life of a remarkable man of God. I am confident that whoever reads his moving life story will be excited by it and drawn closer to the Lord Jesus Christ, the Man in the glory whom Harry Ironside loved fervently and served faithfully and fruitfully for sixty years.

E. S. E.

Merion, Pennsylvania
January 1976

PREFACE TO THE 1946 EDITION

Open to question is the wisdom of writing the biography of a man yet alive, for it is not easy to tell the whole truth about one who is likely to read what has been written. If only the good things are said about him, it might scarcely seem an authentic or full biography. Dr. Ironside himself doubted the wisdom of this work from its first suggestion, and when his consent was finally given to the publishers and the author selected, he wrote me saying, "I certainly do not want the biography written in a way that would glorify this poor sinner. When your name was suggested I felt as though I could trust you to tell (partly) the truth. You will never know the whole—but I do not like to think of your having to bother very much about it."

That the life story of this servant of Christ should be chronicled for others was inevitable, for there is so much in that life. Equally certain, though the author was the only one who knew it then, was the fact that it should be written by me. For a period of five or more years I had prayed that, when the time should come for Dr. Ironside's biography to be recorded, I might be the one selected for the task. I was in no haste to write, for I thought it would best be written after he had been taken from us. At any rate, it was with only slight surprise that I received a long-distance telephone call two years ago inviting me to prepare the work and to complete it by this summer.

As I have said, I seriously doubted the advisability of publishing the biography while Dr. Ironside would be with us. But the coming of the request as an answer to prayer and the realization that it might have a wider distribution and be used for greater good if he were still ministering among us outweighed objections.

Job declared, "Oh . . . that mine adversary had written a book." Certainly one's enemy would say the very worst about him. Equally, one's friend will report as favorably as he can. As his friend I have sought to be wary of this latter fault, and I have also been forewarned by an esteemed brother who, knowing I was beginning the assignment, sent me a copy of J. N. Darby's letter, *On the Praise of Men.* Hence, in writing this book, I have sought to glorify—not a man but the Lord and Saviour of that man who emulates the Apostle Paul in thinking of himself as the chief of sinners.

"Love covereth a multitude of sins," and doubtless my sincere affection for H. A. Ironside may blind my eyes to failures that others may see and of which he himself may know. But even if I were to see these sins of omission or commission—of what value would it be to record them in this volume? All too many of the saints are taking note of the faults in their brethren. I have written of Dr. Ironside as I know him and as the records tell his story. If I have omitted to speak of some unhappy failing, it is because I have not observed it; even if I had, I could see no merit in its being brought to light. For this is not the story of the private life of a man but the record of the public ministry of a servant of Christ and brother in the Lord.

Preparatory to the actual work on the manuscript I read, or reread, several outstanding biographies, religious and secular, as *The Life of Andrew Murray,* J. Du Plessis; *The Life of Madame Guyon,* T. C. Upham; *Memoirs of Robert Murray McCheyne,* Andrew A. Bonar; *The Life of Alexander Whyte, D.D.,* G. F. Barbour; *Yankee from Olympus* (Justice Holmes and His Family), Catherine Drinker Bowen; *Peabody of Groton,* Frank D. Ashburn; and *Dean Briggs,* Rollo Walter Brown. Upon the completion of this interesting and enlightening task I thought I saw the pattern of the biography to be written. It would be filled with Ironside's letters. Gems of wisdom would glisten on every page. The biographee's philosophy of life, his method of sermon preparation, his correspondence with scholars and friends of lesser intellect would compose the book.

Then began my second and more important work of preparation—the reading of the seven thousand pages of diary material which Dr. Ironside has written over many years. These all were penned in his scrawling handwriting. Following that, I perused hundreds of his letters which he had written to institutions and individuals, and which were placed at my disposal by gracious mutual friends. The pattern of the work took on a new shape after this. HAI is not a dreamer, a philosopher, a man of words; he is a man of action.

So it is that I have set down a running narrative, as it were, of a man constantly "on the move" for Christ's sake for more than fifty years. This work could not have been completed without the Lord's help, nor without the tireless cooperation and confidence of its subject, and the gracious and enthusiastic assistance of many others. Acknowledgments are gladly made to all who had a part in the publication of this book, and will be found on another page.

There is doubtless much that I have overlooked in chronicling the lifework of Harry Ironside. What I have written has been done to the end that Christ in all His power and beauty and faithfulness may be seen in what has been wrought through His servant, and that men and women may be encouraged along life's path and incited to fuller yieldedness to the Lord through the record of a faithful steward.

E. S. E.

Skytop, Pennsylvania
September 1945

PART 1

BOYHOOD DAYS

"From a child thou hast known the holy scriptures,
which are able to make thee wise unto salvation
through faith which is in Christ Jesus."

2 TIMOTHY 3:15

"Except the LORD build the house,
they labour in vain that build it. . . .
Lo, children are an heritage of the LORD."

PSALM 127:1,3

1

ROOTS IN DEEP AND SACRED SOIL

On the morning of the fourteenth of October 1876, in a modest home in Toronto, Canada, what had been anticipated as an occasion of greatest blessing appeared to have turned into tragedy. The firstborn son of a godly young couple, John and Sophia Ironside, was set aside as lifeless by the attending physician so that he might give total attention to the mother, who lay weak and dangerously ill. Forty minutes later, to the doctor's astonishment, a nurse who was assisting him detected a pulsebeat in the infant. The physician instructed her to place the child in a hot bath immediately. In a moment the newlyborn baby let out a lusty cry. This book tells the story of that boy who was virtually brought back from the dead—Henry Allan Ironside.

For several generations the Ironsides had been Aberdeenshire farmers. Midway through the nineteenth century, however, an Ironside came along who was disenchanted with the ways of the old country and decided to trust his future to the great new western world across the ocean. So it was that John Williams Ironside departed from the home of his fathers in New Deer, Aberdeenshire, Scotland, and sailed for Canada. His first stopping place in the new country was Fergus,

Ontario, where he was welcomed by another John Ironside, his uncle. A short time later he moved to nearby Elora.

As soon as John found employment in Elora he united with the Baptist Church, for he had been converted to Christ when he was a mere lad. Here he began to develop as a lay preacher. At a social function he met a young lady who sang in the choir of the Methodist Church, Sophia Stafford. The couple became engaged and when John was twenty-three years of age, he and Sophia married. They settled in Toronto, where the young husband obtained a position with the Merchants Bank of Toronto and rose to become a teller.

As a result of happy spiritual fellowship with Christians of their acquaintance, the Ironsides identified themselves with a group known as the Brethren.* Sophia was an ardent soul winner, as was her husband also. While John devoted his evenings to proclaiming Christ at street meetings and in theaters, and Sundays to preaching in the park, Sophia was zealous to bear witness to Christ at every opportunity. Their modest home became a gathering place for many believers. It was also a haven of rest for a number of traveling ambassadors for Christ. John was called "The Eternity Man" because of his custom of inquiring of almost every new acquaintance, "Where will you spend eternity?" He looked forward to and reveled in these visits

---

*Called also, "Plymouth Brethren." Those who assemble and worship according to the principles of these Christians refuse, and in fact disapprove, any name that would distinguish them from all of God's people. They prefer to be spoken of simply as brethren, or believers, or saints, or Christians. In these pages they are referred to as the Brethren (with a capital B) in order to differentiate between them and other brethren in Christ who may have denominational affiliations or other ties.

of his brethren, with whom he spent many hours discussing God's Word and seeking to learn more of Christ.

In 1878 a second son, John Williams Ironside, Jr.* was born to John and Sophia. Three weeks later, bereavement and sorrow came to this little home, for the father of the family became ill with typhoid and before many days passed went to be with his Lord. He was in his twenty-seventh year. Sophia, sustained by the comfort of the Scriptures and secure in God's promises, did not sorrow as others who have no hope. But she would have been less than human, less than the tender and loving wife of a devoted husband, had she shed no tears at his going—not for him, but for her loneliness and for her dear children. These boys were to grow up with no personal recollection of their father, who was held in such happy and revered memory by his brethren throughout Canada and the United States. Many years later, when the older son returned to Toronto as a preacher of the gospel, he was asked again and again if he was the son of John Ironside, The Eternity Man. He found scores of his father's converts continuing in the faith and living for Christ.

John Williams Ironside left burning a light that was still shining to Christ's glory after a quarter of a century.

*John W. Ironside, Jr., served in the Philippine Islands during the Spanish-American War. At its conclusion he settled for a long time in Manila, returning later to Canada, where he died of sleeping sickness.

2

HUSBAND TO THE WIDOW,
FATHER TO THE FATHERLESS

Life was not easy for the widow of The Eternity Man. With his modest salary John Ironside had been able to do little more than care for his family. Therefore Sophia had to undertake immediately the support of her two boys and herself when the second child was scarcely three weeks old. She had one talent that proved useful—her skill with needle and thread. So, like Dorcas of old, she made coats and garments, and "was full of good works and almsdeeds which she did." At length she had more work than she could handle and it became necessary for her to employ others to help her in her small business. But in the early days of her widowhood Sophia's faith in God was tested almost to the breaking point.

Doubtless unaware of Mrs. Ironside's limited means, itinerant Bible teachers continued to look for hospitality in the Ironside home. Sophia welcomed them warmly and urged them to make use of the prophet's chamber. There was one occasion when, quite unexpectedly, John's brother Henry and a friend knocked at the door with their bags in hand, obviously intending to stay at least one night. Sophia was at a loss to know how she would be able to provide even one meal for the pair. It was in such circumstances that her faith was greatest, for then it seemed she needed it most. She fell to her knees and told the Lord all about the visit, asking Him to supply her need according to His promise. Resting in the assurance of the Word, she prepared the first meal for the visitors. When supper was over and they had gone out to a church meeting, she found a ten-dollar bill under one of the plates. With tears in her eyes she offered thanks to God.

Again and again the two boys saw God working in answer to prayer. At one time, when they were about six and four respectively, the larder was nearly empty. Sophia prayed about the family's need and waited for God to act. The answer did not come and one morning the little family went to the breakfast table with nothing to eat and only water to drink.

"We will give thanks, boys," their mother said. Then, closing her eyes, she spoke to God. "Father," she prayed, "Thou hast promised in Thy Word, 'Your bread shall be given you, and your water shall be sure.' We have the water and we thank Thee for it. And now we trust Thee for the bread or something that will take its place." Hardly had she finished praying when the doorbell rang.

At the first sound the boys were on their feet and rushing to the door to see who was there. Was this God answering their mother's prayer? Indeed, it was— though the boys did not think the man at the door looked particularly holy!

"Mrs. Ironside," he said, when she too had reached the door, "I feel very bad. We've been owing you for months for that dress you made for my wife. We've had no money to pay you. But just now we're harvesting our potatoes and we wondered if you'll take a bushel or two on account of the old bill."

"Indeed, I'll be glad to," Sophia answered, and the man brought the baskets into the house.

It did not take long for Mrs. Ironside to get some of those potatoes into the frying pan. "Potatoes and water make a wonderful breakfast," they all thought as Sophia thanked God for His help in the hour of want.

Sophia Ironside tried to teach her boys not only to trust God for material needs but also to honor and know His Word. Praying without ceasing for the salvation of her sons, she was a striking example to them of what it means to have a passion for souls. For although her life was a busy one she did not neglect one of the greatest callings of every child of God—to bear witness concerning Christ. For more than a half century Henry Allan Ironside met and ministered with open-air preachers, mission superintendents, evangelists, missionaries, and Bible teachers across the length and breadth of this continent as well as in Great Britain and Ireland. Yet toward the end of his life he said, "My mother was one of the most earnest personal workers I have ever known."

There was little time for Sophia to go out of the house. Even after she hired other women to help in her dressmaking establishment, she would often work late into the night. The oil lamps were rarely dimmed until after midnight, and at six o'clock in the morning Sophia was again busy with her needle or sewing machine, where her boys would find her when they got up. No, she could not get out to talk to people about their souls, but customers came to the house and a host of them were led to Christ through her faithful witness.

Harry and John Ironside
Ages eight and six, respectively, Toronto, 1884

When a new girl was employed to help in the little shop, it would not be long before Sophia would begin telling her about the Lord. Harry (for so Henry Allan was now called) and John would have fun watching to see how soon the new worker would "get saved." Within a few days after the young lady's arrival John would be likely to say, "Now she's crying." Then the two lively lads would peek into the room where the girl was working, and see her tears flowing. A day or two more might pass, or only a few hours, and one of the brothers would report to the other, "Now she's laughing. I guess she's saved now." For their mother would simply talk to these young women, or to any others who came within conversational range, about their sinful condition and need of a Saviour, and concerning God's gracious provision for them in His Son. Sooner or later they would almost invariably turn to Jesus Christ.

Harry was now well into his eighth year, John in his sixth. Neither of the brothers had had as yet a personal experience with the Lord. Sophia never ceased to pray for their salvation. Throughout his life Harry would recall the substance of her pleas to God for him, "Father, save my boy early. Keep him from ever desiring anything else than to live for Thee. Make him a street preacher like his father. O Father, make him willing to be kicked and cuffed, to suffer shame or anything else for Jesus' sake." And he would think, "My word, but you *are* putting it on thick," and not appreciate it very much.

A person can have religion without being a Christian. That was Harry's experience. From the time he was three years old he memorized Scripture. The first verse that he knew (after the favorite of most youngsters, "Jesus wept") was Luke 19:10, "For the Son of man is come to seek and to save that which was lost." It is a verse that he never forgot, as he did not forget other Scripture passages fixed in his mind in those days. However, Harry knew these first Bible passages by memory, not by heart. His mother asked him again and again whether he was yet saved, and visitors to the home would seek to lead him to the Lord, but always he would evade the question or answer in the negative, and then get away as soon as possible.

One day Harry heard a man say that he had read the whole Bible through every year. Harry liked the idea and decided he would do the same. He completed it for the first time in one year. By the time he was fourteen he had "caught up with himself," as he put it, having finished his fourteenth reading of the Bible in that year. From then on he never failed to read the Book from cover to cover at least once every year until 1948, when advanced cataracts prevented long periods of close reading.

Among the most frequent visitors to the Ironside home in Toronto were two Scottish evangelists who usually traveled together. One of them was very tall and had a long, brown beard. His name was Donald Munro. The other was quite short; his beard was long also, but black, and his eyebrows were bushy and very shaggy. Harry used to enjoy watching him clip them. His name, a very common one, was John Smith; but not so his sobriquet, which was "Hellfire Jack," sufficiently startling to stir the interest of any imaginative lad. This pair, more than any other traveling servants of God, were the bane of Harry's existence. For, every

John Williams Ironside
c. 1880

Donald Munro, c. 1890

General William Booth, c. 1895

morning as they came downstairs for breakfast, and
upon other occasions as well, in season and out of
season, one or the other would ask him: "Harry, my lad,
are you born again?" He would tell them that he went
to Sunday school, memorized Bible verses, and even
gave out tracts, but always the answer would be
something like this, "O laddie, you may give out tracts
and still spend all eternity in hell. 'Ye must be born
again,' Harry boy."

In later years Harry came to think of these two
itinerant preachers as men who carried with them the
atmosphere of eternity, but that was when he had
become a Christian and was himself preaching the
gospel, seeking to win lost souls for Christ. To the boy
of ten they seemed a plague and a scourge, so that one
of his first thoughts, when his mother told her sons
that the family was to leave Toronto to go to California,
was, "Well, *those* two will never get at me again." He
was to learn otherwise.

3

BY FAITH INTO A STRANGE COUNTRY

Toward the end of 1886 Sophia Ironside and her two sons left Toronto and traveled by train to Los Angeles. They were accompanied by the boys' uncle, Allan Ironside. To ten-year-old Harry and his brother John this was a great adventure. They had never even crossed over the border into the United States, and to be going all the way to America's west coast seemed like a dream. There were new faces and new places to see. The two boys never tired of watching the dignified, mustachioed conductors collect and punch tickets, nor of running up and down the aisles of the car. When the train stopped at some station along the way for more than a minute or two, they would get out and stare wide-eyed with admiration and awe at the engine, steaming and puffing as if it was out of breath from its arduous work.

The travelers arrived in Los Angeles on December 12, 1886. They were met with "typical California weather," for the day was bright and balmy. To Sophia this was a token from the Lord that His favor was upon them. In a few days the family of three was settled in a small apartment which friends of the young widow had leased for her, and within a very short time she was busy again at her sewing machine.

Almost immediately Harry and John began to attend Sunday school. They had to go a long way to do this, for there was none nearby. Frequently on Sunday afternoons the small family would walk somewhere in the city and Harry, even though he was not yet eleven years old, was shocked and strangely stirred at the ungodly things he observed. Saloons and gambling houses were wide open and doing business on the Lord's day. Intoxication was prevalent.

Harry decided that he himself must start a neighborhood Sunday school. Calling together the boys and girls he knew, he talked with them about it and persuaded the boys to go out and collect as many burlap bags as they could find. Then he organized the girls into a sewing club. In a very short time the Sunday school began, housed in a burlap tent that would accommodate nearly a hundred people. There was no teacher, so Harry began to teach. The average attendance during the first year was sixty—mostly boys and girls, but some few adults also. When Harry could think of nothing else to talk about, he would always revert to Isaiah 53. He assumed that since he had been reared in a Christian home, he was a Christian. He felt that everyone should know the Bible and considered himself a missionary among these people to teach it to them. He was rather proud of his religion and familiarity with the Book about which others knew so little, and nothing pleased him better than to have an adult pat his head or shoulder and say, "God bless this little preacher." Like Timothy, from a child he had known the Holy Scriptures; but unlike Timothy, he had not yet come to the place where the Scriptures made him "wise unto salvation through faith which is in Christ Jesus."

In Harry's twelfth year something occurred that unquestionably was to have a determining effect upon his whole career. For in 1888 Dwight L. Moody came to Los Angeles for his great campaign there.

The meetings were held in Hazzard's Pavilion, which had a seating capacity of 8,000. It was filled to the brim every night. Harry went alone the first night and arrived after a song service conducted by George C. Stebbins had begun. There was not a seat to be had, even for a little chap. But being a determined and observant youngster, he continued looking for a place to sit. He went up to the first gallery, and then to the second. There he noticed another boy of approximately his own age lying at an angle of about forty-five degrees in a troughlike girder that extended from the second gallery to the apex of the roof. That seemed like a good idea to Harry, so he chose another girder and, climbing into it, crawled to an excellent vantage point where he could see everything and hear quite well.

The singing thrilled him, but the great moment came when Mr. Moody rose and stepped to the podium. He was a short, thickset man with a large head, a gray beard, and a somewhat short neck. To Harry, looking down from the rafter, it seemed as if the evangelist had no neck at all. When Moody began to speak, it was in a crisp and efficient way, with a New England twang which was strange to the lad—a way which an old Scotch lady said "did no even hae a holy tone to it."

The text of Moody's message that first night was Daniel 5:27, "Thou art weighed in the balances, and art found wanting." He told the story of the sin and doom of Belshazzar with convincing power. Among those in the audience who were deeply moved was young Harry

Ironside. High up there in the girder, while the message was still in progress, the boy lifted his heart to God and prayed, "Lord, help me some day to preach to crowds like these, and to lead souls to Christ." Forty-two years after that prayer was uttered H. A. Ironside, having preached often to similar crowds and, by God's grace, having led multitudes to know Jesus Christ, became the pastor of the Chicago church that D. L. Moody founded.

Not only did Harry remember the text of the message, but the sermon itself burned into his heart also. Reading it some years later, he said, "I was surprised to find how little of it I had forgotten through the years." Three things about Moody's preaching impressed themselves upon the lad that night, although he was still an unsaved, if religious, boy. Moody spoke for only thirty-five minutes; he quoted many Scripture passages, illuminating them with moving illustrations that were homely and tender; and he pressed upon his hearers the importance of definite personal faith in the Lord Jesus Christ as Saviour.

One night Harry went to a meeting with his mother and some of her friends. They arrived at the Pavilion early and were able to obtain seats quite near the front. This was the boy's first good view of the evangelist and he thought, "He isn't very handsome." Then Moody began to preach. His text was "Sowing and Reaping." To the young lad the preacher's face as he spoke seemed to light up in such a way that he was beautiful to look upon.

As the party was going home from the meeting one of the men remarked, "Moody seems just a very ordinary man. I've heard many better preachers."

Harry (*center*) with His Mother and Brother
in the Year of His Conversion, age twelve
Los Angeles, c. 1888

"Yes," said Sophia, "but Mr. Moody wins souls."

It was this about Dwight L. Moody more than anything else that engraved itself upon the mind of the twelve-year-old boy. It was not a remarkable eloquence or a superior preaching ability that made Moody the success he was, but rather the fact that he was dominated by the Spirit of God and preached with a heart that understood and felt for the needs of his audiences.

Young Ironside continued his active religious work. It was good work but lacked power because the worker was as yet unsaved. True, at times he was in anxiety about his soul, but he did nothing about it. He was conscious, though, of a restraining hand that kept him from many of the questionable practices that some of his friends, not a few being older than he, enjoyed. He was guilty of sin all right, but not that kind.

By this time the Ironsides had moved into a house where Sophia, as she had done in Toronto, presided over a small dressmaking establishment. Harry was now fourteen years old and a senior in grammar school. When he came home from school one afternoon his mother greeted him on the porch. She was very excited.

"Harry, who do you suppose is here?" she asked. Because she seemed so pleased, Harry thought it must be Uncle Henry. Sophia told him to guess again; but without waiting for him to utter another word she gave him the answer, "It's Mr. Munro." One of Harry's bearded tormentors of Toronto had caught up with him at last!

The boy went into the house knowing what was coming, and come it did.

"Well, well, Harry lad," Donald Munro greeted him, "how you have grown! And are you born again yet, my boy?"

Harry hung his head and blushed with embarrassment. He did not like it any better than he had in former days and hardly knew what to say.

Feeling sorry for the boy, Uncle Allan, who had come calling with Mr. Munro, said, "Oh, Harry himself preaches now," referring of course to Harry's Sunday school.

"You are preaching, and yet you don't know that you're born again!" Mr. Munro ejaculated in astonishment. "Go and get your Bible, lad." And Harry, who was glad of any excuse to get out of the room, fled up the stairs. He knew he had to come down again, but he delayed as long as he could. When finally he could stay away no longer without being rude, he descended with his Bible in his hand.

First thing, Mr. Munro asked Harry to turn to Romans 3:19. The boy did, and Mr. Munro said, "Now read it aloud." Harry complied: "Now we know that what things soever the law saith, it saith to them who are under the law: that every mouth may be stopped, and all the world may become guilty before God." He had scarcely begun reading when he knew why his catechist had chosen the passage.

"Harry, lad, have you ever been there?" Mr. Munro asked him.

"What do you mean?" the boy countered.

"Well," said the man, "I understand that you have got your mouth pretty wide open trying to preach to other people. When God makes a preacher, He stops his mouth first and then, when that person sees his lost

condition, God leads him to put his trust in the Lord
Jesus. When he trusts, he is born of God and his soul is
saved. Then God opens his mouth. You've been putting
the cart before the horse, haven't you?"

"Maybe I have," Harry replied.

The conversation ended. But young Ironside was
never able to dislodge from his mind the telling words
of Donald Munro. In his spirit of concern the devil
planted rebellion. Within a few weeks Harry gave up
his Sunday school, for he felt that his soul was lost. If
he were unsaved, he had no right to open his mouth for
God. He knew that there was a way to overcome this
hindrance to his doing the work he loved so much, but
he was unwilling to yield himself to the Lord. It was
not that he was ashamed of the gospel. He had preached it often, had even been taunted for this at times. It
was just that he would not be forced, he thought, to go
through the steps necessary to become a Christian. He
had been a leader and example among his fellows. He
could not begin at the beginning and confess his sins
and Christ as his Saviour and Lord. He was ripe for
Satan's darts and the devil tempted him with the guile
that has brought many souls low. "If you are lost," he
suggested to the unhappy lad, "if you are unfit to
preach the Bible, why not enjoy all the things of the
world from which you have refrained all this time?"

For the first time in his life Harry Ironside began to
enter into activities that he had always considered
worldly, even sinful. One thing bothered him,
however—he was never happy doing these things.
Nevertheless he continued living in this way for about
six months. One night in February 1890 he went to a
party of young people, most of whom were older than

he. After a little while he edged over to a punch bowl, more to get in a corner by himself than to have a drink. As he stood there some Scripture came to his mind. It was hardly a portion a boy of fourteen would recall, in fact few boys of that age would have read it, but the words stood out before him as if they were embossed on the wall. The passage that the Holy Spirit brought to Harry's mind was Proverbs 1:23-28:

> Turn you at my reproof: behold, I will pour out my spirit unto you, I will make known my words unto you. Because I have called, and ye refused; I have stretched out my hand, and no man regarded; But ye have set at nought all my counsel, and would none of my reproof: I also will laugh at your calamity; I will mock when your fear cometh; When your fear cometh as desolation, and your destruction cometh as a whirlwind; when distress and anguish cometh upon you. Then shall they call upon me, but I will not answer; they shall seek me early, but they shall not find me.

Young Ironside was dumfounded. Every word seemed to cut into his heart. He saw, as he had never seen before, his guilt before God, the hardness of his heart in deliberately refusing to put his trust in Jesus Christ, who died for him. He recognized that he, Harry Ironside, had all along been preferring his own will above the will of the Lord. He looked around him. What was he doing here? Everything seemed so hollow, so frivolous, his friends so oblivious of the fact that the judgment of Almighty God was hanging over all of them like the sword of Damocles. He himself was the worst of all, for he knew more about God and His Word than any of them. As soon as he could, he left the party and hurried home, for he wanted to get to his room and be alone.

It was after midnight when Harry reached home. He removed his shoes so as not to be heard along the hall to his bedroom, but Sophia was the kind of mother who cannot sleep when her children are out. She knew he was there. Doubtless she had been praying for him. She called him to her room, but he hurried on, saying, "I'm sorry to be so late." He knew one thing for certain: he wanted to "get saved," and he wanted it right now.

Entering his room the boy fell on his knees and prayed, "Lord, save me." Then the question came to his mind, "What am I praying for? To be saved? Is God unwilling to save me? Doesn't the Bible say He's not willing that any should perish? Am I praying for something God has wanted to do all along?"

Remembering that Mr. Munro had asked him to read Romans 3, Harry turned to that chapter. He understood most of it but was not yet satisfied. Then he recalled that his mother had often remarked that the place to begin with God is at John 3 and Romans 3. So now he leafed through to the third chapter of John. He knew it by memory but read it just the same. It had never before made a very deep impression upon him, but it did this time. When he came to verse 14, telling of Moses lifting up the brazen serpent in the wilderness, it struck him vividly that just as the Israelites had to look at the serpent for life, so he must look at the Lord Jesus Christ. He examined John 3:16.

"Lord," he said, "it says here that whoever believes in Thy Son has everlasting life. And again here, in verse 18, that he that believes in Him is not condemned but has everlasting life. But, Lord, though I believe it, and what Thou hast said must be true, I don't feel any different. I ought to feel different, shouldn't I? But God, I take Thee at Thy Word. I believe that Thou dost now save my soul because I trust in the Lord Jesus Christ."

The distraught lad thought surely that then, after he had told God that he was taking Him at His Word, some great and new emotion would overpower him. But nothing happened. He began all over again. Again he reached the same conclusion. So once more he talked with the Lord.

"Lord, Thy Word says, 'He that believeth on Him is not condemned: but he that believeth not is condemned already, because he hath not believed in the name of the only begotten Son of God.' I'm not in the last class—among those that don't believe," he said, "therefore I'm not condemned. 'He that believeth on Him is not condemned'—that is I, for Thou dost say so. Lord, I thank Thee for that, and I rest on it. That will do. O God, I thank Thee for Thy love and for the gift of Thy Son. Yes, I take Him now; I trust Him as my Saviour—believing Thy Word, I know that I have eternal life." He rose from his knees and began the walk of faith. God could not lie. Harry knew he was saved according to the Word. "Harry lad" had been born again.

PART 2

IN THE SALVATION ARMY

"Prove all things; hold fast that which is good."
1 THESSALONIANS 5:21

"He that winneth souls is wise."

PROVERBS 11:30

4

JOYFUL READINESS TO PUBLISH
GLAD TIDINGS

From the moment of his conversion Harry Ironside wanted to speak to others about Christ. He thought he ought to tell his mother first but, like many other people then and now, he found it difficult to confide in the one dearest to him. Breakfast passed the next morning and he was silent. On his way to school he was sure that when he saw his chum he would tell him of this wonderful thing that had happened to him. For some reason he could not define, he was unable to say a word. A full day slipped by. His new life seemed to be bubbling inside him, but it stayed there. It was one of the few days in his more than half-century of Christian experience that Ironside failed to speak out for the Lord. The next day was Saturday. Harry received permission from his mother to attend a Salvation Army meeting that was to be held nearby in the evening.

The Salvation Army was young in those days and zealous to win souls for Christ. To Harry they seemed just the right kind of Christians. He recalled the words of St. Paul that "all that will live godly in Christ Jesus shall suffer persecution." Certainly, he thought, the Salvationists suffer ridicule, and that is a form of persecution. There was no doubt that they preached the gospel faithfully and fearlessly. Harry remembered how his mother had prayed about him back there in Toronto, "Make him a street preacher like his father. Make him willing to be cuffed and kicked, to suffer shame or anything else for Jesus' sake." It was no wonder that this lad, as soon as he became a Christian, seemed somehow to be drawn to the Army.

The street meeting was already underway when Harry arrived. The Salvation Army captain who was speaking was a familiar figure to the youngster, who had seen him on several occasions of a similar nature. He was a diamond in the rough who looked more like a lion than a jewel, with his long and shaggy mane and a mouth that seemed to the lad to have a hundred large teeth. More than once Harry had heard him tell the story of his conversion, which he did this night—how, while kneeling at a penitent bench in a Salvation Army hall, he had emptied his pockets of a knife, a gun, a pack of cards, and a pipe, and throwing them on the floor in front of him, had cried out, "Lord, if You can make anything out of me, do it!"

Harry could hardly wait for the captain to finish speaking. After what seemed to the lad like an age, he *did* stop and the impatient boy stepped forward and asked, "Captain, may I give my testimony?"

"Are you saved, lad?" the captain responded, sounding very much like Mr. Munro.

Harry's reaction this time was far different from what it had been with Mr. Munro.

"Oh, yes," he said firmly and joyfully.

"How do you know?" was the next question.

"Because I have trusted in the Lord Jesus Christ as my Saviour."

"When was that?"

"The day before yesterday," Harry said.

"Then fire away!"

And fire away Harry did, preaching his first sermon as a Christian. His text was Isaiah 53:6, "All we like sheep have gone astray; we have turned every one to his own way; and the LORD hath laid on Him the iniquity of us all." He was well into his message when he noticed a group of young people coming to the edge of the surrounding crowd—the friends who had been at the party on Thursday night when God had spoken to him so definitely. Although he was nonplused momentarily and his tongue seemed too big for his mouth, he went right on speaking. It was with utmost difficulty that he was able to continue. But on he went, expounding the Scripture as clearly as he could and giving his testimony. The crisis passed. He had been speaking now for about thirty minutes. Pulling the boy's coattail the captain muttered, "Boy, we should have been in the hall twenty minutes ago. You'll have to tell us the rest some other time."* So Harry stopped.

The next day Harry went to the regular Sunday afternoon services at the Army's hall. He gave his testimony there and, after the meeting, an old black man came up to him and said, "I want to talk to you. You've got something I've wanted a long time. I don't know what it is, but I want it." Despite the fact that the man was five times Harry's age, the young man led him over to a park known as the Plaza. The two of them sat down on a bench and Harry opened his Bible to the

---

*In his book on Isaiah, published posthumously in 1952 (Loizeaux Brothers), H. A. Ironside alludes briefly to this incident and adds, "I have been trying to tell the rest all through the years since, but I never get beyond this text."

passages his mother had told him were the places to begin with God—John 3, Romans 3, and Isaiah 53—and explained them to the old man.

"Does this mean," the black man asked, "that even though I've sinned a lot, Jesus died for me? I just need to trust Him and I'll be saved?"

"That's what it means," Harry assured him.

"I wish I'd known that fifty years ago," the man said.

"Well, you know it now, don't you?" Harry replied. Upon a nodded assent from the old man, Harry said to him, "Let's get down on our knees and thank God for it." Then and there in an open park the black man and the white boy knelt down at the bench where they had been sitting and thanked God for salvation through Jesus Christ, praising Him specifically for the salvation of the old man that day. Harry Ironside had won his first convert to Christ.

Still the boy had not told his mother about his new birth, his new-found life. However, on that same Sunday night Sophia went down to a rescue mission where she played the organ regularly. After services it was her custom to deal with some of the visitors about their souls. On this occasion she approached a man and asked if he would like to know Jesus Christ as his Saviour. He said something to her about the mission's failure to reach his heart the way the little preacher up at the corner did.

"What little preacher?" Sophia asked.

"Oh, I don't know his name," the man told her. "He's a little bit of a feller. When he talks, something happens to me. I feel different from what I do here at the mission."

Sophia was not slow in putting two and two

together. She asked some more questions and, when she and Harry had both gotten home that night, she inquired, "Harry, did you go to that street meeting last night?"

"Yes, I did," he answered.

"Did you preach?"

"Well, I gave my testimony, if you call that preaching."

"But," Sophia continued, "what right do you have to testify? Nobody has a right to do that unless he's saved."

"But I am saved, Mother."

"You are? When did that happen?"

"Last Thursday night," Harry said, and then he told her all about it.

When he had finished, his mother asked him: "Why didn't you tell me before, Harry?"

"Well, I wanted to see if you noticed any change in me since I've been saved."

"I did think I noticed a difference, Harry," she said, and hugged him. It was "a time to weep, and a time to laugh." Mother and son did a little of each as they thanked God for His faithfulness in answering her prayers for her older boy.

Another exciting event took place at about that time which was also to have a lasting effect on the future of the Ironside family. Sophia married again. Her new husband was William D. Watson. Like Harry's father, Watson was an Aberdeenshireman from Old Deer. He owned a ranch in Monte Vista (later called Sunland) and also a two-room house in Los Angeles, which he spoke of as his "shack." Before his marriage to Sophia, this small house was his headquarters in the winter. After the wedding, he moved into the Ironside home and, about a year later, a daughter, Lillian, was born to the Watsons. To have a sister was a great event in the lives of the two boys.

When a circumstance arose that required the Watsons to move down to the ranch, they took John and Lillian with them. Harry, who had found a part-time job with a shoemaker, was earning sufficient money to take care of himself in a modest way and wanted to remain in Los Angeles until his graduation. He was quite mature for his age, so the Watsons arranged for him to stay in Watson's shack for the few weeks left before graduation.

Young Ironside's burning urgency was to preach the gospel. Because of this, he made a decision then that he regretted the rest of his life—not to pursue his education further but to get a full-time position so that he could devote every spare hour to preaching. He was able to find a job at the Lamson Photo Studio in the city. The parents of one of his school chums agreed to take him into their home in the outskirts of the city as a boarder for a modest fee. There he settled.

Night after night Harry attended one of the Salvation Army meetings in Los Angeles. He spoke so frequently that he became well known as "The Boy Preacher." Being a very young Christian, this title pleased his vanity. It was only later that he came to realize that his vanity was really nothing else than pride, one of the sins that God hates. But he was exceedingly happy in those days, finding many opportunities to exercise his tremendous energy and zeal for the Lord.

Whereas Harry Ironside's formal education ceased

at the age of fourteen, he never ceased educating himself. Most of his life he was an insatiable reader. By the time he was fifteen he possessed a good library which made up in quality what it lacked in quantity. Titles by Dickens, Thackeray, Longfellow, Kant, Plato, and other philosophers and poets were conspicuous on his bookshelves. While still in his twenties he had read *The Pilgrim's Progress* more than twenty times.

As a diversion Harry had studied the Chinese language during his last two years in grammar school. He had met a Chinese physician who wanted to increase his knowledge of English, so the two of them spent two hours together every week, each learning a new tongue. Interest in this old oriental language remained with Ironside throughout his life. Whereas others might doodle on scraps of paper, Harry traced out intricate Chinese characters as a form of relaxation. The flyleaf of one of his Bibles illustrates this habit of his.

However, neither the pursuit of knowledge nor the following of a trade deterred Harry from what he considered his calling. Photography was to him what shoemaking was to William Carey, the great missionary to India, who, when as a young man in England he was asked his business, replied, "My business is to serve the Lord; I make shoes to pay expenses." Every moment that Harry could find he employed in active gospel work. When he was not attending Salvationist meetings, either on the street or in their halls, he would be giving out tracts or holding street meetings of his own.

It was only a few months after his graduation from school that young Ironside identified himself on a part-

Harry Ironside
age fourteen
A Salvation Army Soldier
1890

Captain Read
of the
Salvation Army
and
Lieutenant Ironside
age sixteen, 1892

time basis with the Salvation Army, which was then at its spiritual zenith. Its leaders had one purpose—to go out after lost men and women, and to lead them to Christ. Harry's ardor to reach the unsaved matched theirs and he began his witness with them with such boldness that before long he was given the rank of junior sergeant major.

In Harry's sixteenth year the Army's Captain James Armstrong invited him to come down to San Diego to help him there. At the same time Armstrong urged him to enroll in the San Diego cadet school for training requisite for all Salvation Army personnel desirous of gaining full officership. He accepted the offer and immediately resigned his position with the Lamson Photo Studio.

On the day that Harry Ironside left his job to enter into full-time work with the Salvation Army, his employer, J. F. Dando, said, "A good photographer has been spoiled to make a poor preacher."

5

TAKE HEED UNTO THYSELF
AND UNTO THE DOCTRINE

Every Sunday morning in San Diego the Salvation Army held their "holiness meetings." Young Ironside attended regularly and listened to men and women who claimed to have received a second blessing from God the Holy Spirit. There were various names for the experience; but whatever the name, those who testified about receiving it would speak of having perfect sanctification, of having been cleansed from inbred sin, of having attained a higher life of perfect love. According to this doctrine, salvation consists of original cleansing from past sins and release from their penalty, both of which are received by faith in Jesus Christ and His atoning sacrifice. So far so good, but according to the proponents of the "holiness" teaching, even though justification is a free gift from God and is bestowed by Him upon a believing sinner as a result of the redemptive work of Christ, that justified position in God's sight is forfeited if that same believer falls into sin. Consequently, so the "holiness" people say, he needs a second work of grace known as sanctification. He who would enjoy this state must experience three things: conviction of the need; complete surrender of

everything to God—desires, hopes, and ambitions—
laying all on the altar; and appropriation by faith of
the incoming Holy Spirit, who would then burn out all
passions and destroy all inbred sin. To reach this state,
it was taught, would cause a person to be as pure as
Adam was before he fell.

Ironside had no doubt about the sincerity of those
who bore witness that they were recipients of this
special work of grace, never for a moment questioning
the genuineness of their experiences. To hear these
people, most of whom were affiliated with the Salvation Army, tell of not having sinned for many years in
thought, word, or deed; to be told that bad tempers had
been quelled and rooted out, evil thoughts banished
forever, and wicked desires absolutely destroyed—all
this awakened in the young man an overwhelming ardor for a similar experience.

Harry was obliged to confess to himself that up to
this time he could not claim freedom from sinful
thoughts and deeds. When he was first saved, at the
age of fourteen, he had thought that none on earth
could have more joy than he had, none could be as close
to God as he then felt himself to be. But he certainly
could not say that sin had been eradicated from his life.
He well remembered one occasion, within a few weeks
after he had been born again, when, in the heat of
anger, he struck his young brother so viciously that he
knocked him to the ground. Instantly his own soul had
been filled with shame, an emotion that only increased
when John shouted in derision, "A fine Christian you
are! Why don't you go down to the Army now and
testify? Tell them what a saint you are!"

Harry remembered now how humiliated and broken

in spirit he had been, how he had rushed into the house and locked himself in his room, confessing his sin to God. In anguish he pled with God to forgive him, and then he also asked John to forgive him. But in that experience he had been made aware that, although he was a Christian as surely as God's Word is true, he was certainly capable of sinning.

What was this second work of grace the Salvationists were claiming? How could he obtain it? He began to pray for and seek it in every conceivable way. Anything that gave even the slightest indication of lack of surrender on his part, he sought to put away. He gave up friends who seemed not to be perfected in holiness, and refrained from every sort of amusement. He even laid aside all his books, except the Bible and certain holiness writings, in his zeal to obtain the blessing that these others had. He felt that what they could receive and enjoy was for him, too, provided he would only meet the conditions.

To that end and after weeks of prayer, Harry made up his mind one Saturday during a fortnight's mission in Los Angeles, to get away into some secluded spot and there, free from interruption and unhampered by interference of any kind, wait upon God and hold on to Him in faith until he received "the blessing of perfect love." At eleven o'clock that night he took a train from the city to a country place about twelve miles distant and, leaving the train, walked along the road for a space and then turned off it to an empty arroyo. Falling on his knees beneath a sycamore tree, he besought God for hours, with tears and supplications, that He would show him anything within himself that hindered the blessing. There came to his mind certain private matters and, after struggling for a long time against conviction about them, he finally sobbed out in all sincerity: "Lord, I give up all—everything, every person, every enjoyment that would hinder my living for Thee alone. Now, I pray Thee, give me the blessing."

Insofar as the ardent young man was able to understand it, at that moment he was fully yielded to God. Unstrung by the long and fervent agonizing in prayer, he fell to the ground in a faint. In a few moments he was conscious of an ecstasy such as he had never before experienced. This surely is the coming of the Holy Spirit into my heart, he thought. This is what I've been seeking—and rising to his knees he cried to God, "Lord, I believe Thou dost come in. Thou dost cleanse me from all sin, and purify me from it. I claim it, Lord. The work is done. I am sanctified by Thy blood. Thou dost make me holy. I believe! I believe!"

He was so unutterably happy, so full of praise to God, that he forgot his weariness and rose to his feet and began to sing aloud. He must get back and tell others of this experience. The trains had stopped running, for it was then three-thirty in the morning. So he set out to walk to Los Angeles in order to get into the city in time for the early morning prayer meeting. Tired as he had been and still was, it seemed as nothing to him in the light of his new-found joy, and he stepped off the miles as if gliding on a cloud, arriving at the hall in time to give his testimony of the glorious experience. He was literally intoxicated with joyous emotion. For were his troubles not ended now? Did he not have complete sanctification? Was his heart not wholly pure?

The weeks that followed were filled with happy days. Harry continued to seek lost souls, but even while he was doing so he lived as if in a dream. Nothing was altered in his message to the unsaved, to whom he preached Christ crucified and risen again. But there was a change in his testimonies as he gave them night after night. He himself began to notice it as quickly perhaps as others did. Heretofore he had always held up the person of Christ; now he was lifting up the person of Harry Ironside. He pointed to himself as an example for others to emulate—an example of surrender and holiness.

It was not long, however, before he began to be conscious that all was not well. There crept into his heart desires toward evil, some of which he had never experienced before. But he was temporarily anaesthetized by the assurance that this was but temptation, and temptation is not sin. For a while this explanation seemed to give him some peace, but not for long: soon he observed himself slipping onto a much lower plane of living than he had marked out for himself. He noticed, too, that others who were "sanctified" were living on an equally low level with himself, if not actually lower. The rapture of his earlier experience had left him entirely. Doubts began to creep in and, with the doubts, fears. When he was busy proclaiming the gospel and seeing men and women come to Christ, he was happy; but when he allowed himself to think of his spiritual life and weigh it, he became extremely depressed. Oh well, doubts and depression were the devil's darts and were not sin, he thought. Lust was not sin unless it was yielded to, and as long as he committed no overt acts, he was still "sanctified."

It was in such a state that Cadet Ironside entered the Oakland Training Garrison in Oakland preparatory to becoming an officer in the Salvation Army. The trouble of spirit that he had before experienced increased there under strict discipline and enforced association with other young men of varied degrees of spiritual discernment, men who came from all walks of life, some of whom displayed very little "sanctification" indeed. As the term of six months' training neared its close, Harry was in a miserable state. He thought that he was a backslider, at least, and feared that he might be lost eternally.

Twice he slipped out at night to a lonely place and sought to discover the mind of the Lord about these matters, praying all night. He asked God not to take His Holy Spirit from him and to cleanse him afresh from inbred sin. As he had done in the arroyo on the occasion of his first wondrous experience in a deserted place, he claimed the answers to his prayers by faith, and returned to his work refreshed. But shortly thereafter he would again be seized with doubts, spurred by his awareness of having even lately sinned in word and thought, and sometimes in deed. Extreme remorse would inevitably follow.

At length came the happy day of his commissioning, when he was made a lieutenant in the Salvation Army. He spent the preceding night in prayer, for he felt that he must not teach others unless he himself was completely "sanctified." Freed now from confinement and from the sense of restraint, at sixteen years of age a full-fledged officer in the stalwart Salvation Army, the glorious army of the Lord, Lieutenant Ironside went down to San Bernardino, for the most part a happy young man. Conscientious almost to a fault, he became a strong advocate of "second blessing" teaching and even prayed that his dear mother might experience "the cleansing from inbred sin."

It did not occur to Harry that Sophia, who had been a devoted Christian before he was born, knew her own heart too well to talk of sinlessness or to expect it in this life.

6

ISAIAH FIFTY-THREE AGAIN

Lieutenant Ironside's arrival in San Bernardino was in the middle of a Salvation Army evangelistic campaign, where he was sent to assist Captain John Read. The meetings in the Salvation Hall had been going on for some days. Already there had been a number of remarkable conversions to Christ and the hall was being filled to capacity every night.

Among the regular attendants whom the lieutenant noticed was a handsome, blond young man. He appeared to be immensely interested in all that was said, and on several occasions Harry tried to intercept him at the end of a service, but the young man slipped away before Ironside could catch him.

One night, however, this man was late for the meeting and the only seat he could find was in the front row. Lieutenant Ironside said to himself, "You won't get away this time, my friend," and the moment the benediction was pronounced he hurried down from the platform and seized the young man by the arm, inviting him to sit down for a moment. In the conversation that followed it developed that this man, who had been brought up in England and was quite evidently well educated, made no profession of being a Christian. In fact, after some probing on Harry's part, the stranger admitted to having been an atheist at one time, but more recently an agnostic.

It seems that an intimate friend of the blond Englishman had been converted to Christ within the past several months, and the change in his life was so apparent and so great, including complete victory over a seemingly invincible drinking habit of many years, that the young man telling the story confessed to his interrogator that he now realized that nothing less than a supernatural power could have effected this amazing transformation in his friend. Therefore he himself, the blond chap reiterated, could no longer be an atheist.

Ironside asked him whether he had read the Bible. Yes, he had read some of it recently, but not a great deal. The four Gospels? Yes, he found it difficult to accept the miraculous.

"Well, how about the Old Testament?" Harry inquired.

In response, the young man said that, not only had he read some of it but also that he was impressed by the writing of the Prophet Isaiah.

"If I could become a Christian by believing Isaiah," he said, "I think I might be persuaded to do so."

This was the opportunity Harry had been looking for, and he took advantage of it. Opening his Bible, he said, "I'm going to read a passage from Isaiah. I'll read about an unidentified man, and when I've finished, I want you to tell me his name."

"Why, that would be impossible!" the young man answered. "I don't know the Bible that well."

"Try it and see," the lieutenant said and began reading at Isaiah 53, verse 1, and continued through the whole chapter. When he had finished reading, he looked up into the other's face and asked: "Tell me now, of whom was Isaiah speaking?"

Eagerly the young man exclaimed, "Let me read it for myself, sir!" to the officer who was at least ten years his junior.

Ironside handed him the Bible and watched as he read. He saw him furtively wipe away a tear. When the reading was finished, he remained quiet for a moment, and then said, "I must confess, it has to be—Jesus."

"You're right," Lieutenant Ironside replied. "Now let me give you a nut for skeptics to crack. That description of the life and death of Jesus Christ was written seven hundred years before the Saviour was born. Can you account for this?"

"Can you prove that?" the self-professed agnostic asked. "How do you know it was written so long ago?"

It was here that some of young Ironside's extensive reading bore fruit.

"Of course," he said, "I'm accepting the record that Isaiah lived in the eighth century before Christ. If you reject the record of the Scriptures, I can't prove it. But," he continued, "there is something else in connection with the Scriptures that anyone who cares to investigate may prove to himself. The portion which we read a moment ago was translated from the Hebrew language into Greek and placed in the library of Ptolemy Philadelphus in Alexandria about 230 years before the birth of Christ. It must have existed in Hebrew for some time before being translated into Greek. At any rate, it was just as great a miracle for the prophecy to have been written in Greek over two centuries before Christ's birth as it was for it to have existed seven centuries prior to His coming to earth. How could Isaiah have known of these things except by divine inspiration?"

At this, the strange young man rose to his feet and, without a word, hurried from the hall.

Several nights passed before the Englishman appeared again at the hall. He walked confidently down the aisle and seated himself in the front row, looking directly at Harry. The moment the meeting was opened for testimonies, he rose to his feet and spoke with boldness.

"My friends, I want to tell you tonight that after years of unbelief God has revealed to me, through Isaiah 53, Jesus Christ as my Saviour. I have read that chapter over and over again during the last few days and nights. I have been greatly troubled, feeling that I have sinned too greatly and too often for God ever to forgive me. But tonight I'm sure that He has done so, through Jesus' death for me.

"There's a confession I've got to make. Upon my graduation, as a civil engineer from Cambridge University in England, I was one of the first to be sent out to Palestine to survey the railroad from Jaffa to Jerusalem. I can't tell you how strongly I was affected by all I saw in that country. The very stones of the ground seemed to rise up against my unbelief and to declare the Bible to be true. But I comforted myself by saying that it was all superstition. I refused to believe.

"One day a group of us engineers was taken by a guide to Gordon's Calvary, that skull-like hill where General Gordon claimed that Christ was crucified. As we stood on that knoll it came to me that this was the place where Christianity began—and to me, Christianity was a delusion. My wrath was aroused. I burst forth in uncontrolled blasphemy against God and Christ, in cursing beyond description, so that even my ungodly friends were frightened and literally fled from the spot. Some told me afterward that they thought God would strike me dead then and there, so fierce was my desecration of that sacred place, so horrible my blasphemy against God.

"But, oh, my friends, I have lived to learn in the last few days that the One whom I cursed on Calvary's hill was wounded for my transgressions, and bruised for my iniquities; the chastisement of my peace was upon Him, and with His stripes I am healed."

The young man could say no more. He fell to his seat in tears, but the hearts of those who heard him were filled with joy. So, indeed, was Harry's. His first sermon as a Christian had been from the fifty-third chapter of Isaiah, and his first convert as a lieutenant came about through that same passage.

7

FINDING CHRIST TO BE ALL
AND IN ALL

With the spirit of immediacy characteristic of the Salvation Army in those days, Lieutenant Ironside pressed on in his evangelistic ministry. Not by any means was every conversion to Christ as dramatic as the one recounted in the preceding chapter, but almost every conversion was a genuine one. Ironside moved north and south in California in places like Los Gatos, Red Bluff, Stockton, and Sacramento, as well as in some of the larger cities, calling upon men and women to turn to Jesus Christ and give Him the lordship of their lives. Demands for his ministry widened. He rose rapidly to the rank of captain and, in addition to his responsibilities as head of the corps, began an indefatigable schedule of speaking about 400 times a year, a program that lasted for about a half century. A highlight of his second year as an officer was his assignment as orderly to General William Booth, when the founder of the Salvation Army visited San Francisco for several days. As fervent and tireless as Harry had been as a soul winner up to that time, General Booth impressed upon him, as never before, the imperative of reaching the lost with the gospel of Christ.

Because of his varied and ceaseless activities, Captain Ironside found little time to reflect upon spiritual matters unrelated to his primary charge—evangelism. He put off giving further consideration to the holiness doctrine that was being taught by many of his associates and was expected of him. He enjoyed thoroughly the work he was engaged in and endured gladly for Christ's sake whatever privations and hardships were his lot. He felt satisfied that he was trying to demonstrate in his own life the doctrine of "perfect love" both Godward and manward, and consequently he was reasonably certain that he was making his own salvation secure by his sacrifices and works of righteousness. It was easy to delude himself and to postpone thinking deeply about the problem. It seemed better at the time to go along with his brethren, he thought; furthermore to maintain the status quo would be less disruptive to the peace of the corps than to air his doubts and his consciousness of being far less "holy" than his fellow soldiers supposed him to be.

However, during his third year as an officer, dormant misgivings began to awaken and disturb Harry in such a way that he knew he must face up to the issue, come what may. He did not dare to talk freely to those closest to him in the work, officers of lesser rank than he as well as regular Salvation Army soldiers, lest in disclosing his own uncertainties he should do irreparable harm to them. They would look upon him as a backslider, and his influence, which had in the past been helpful, might cease.

For several months Captain Ironside continued his work in this unhappy condition. To add to his misery, another, a young woman officer with whom he was

Captain Harry Ironside of the Salvation Army
age twenty, 1896

"keeping company" at that time and with whom at length he shared his doubts, was unable to stand the strain and eventually fell into the maze of spiritualism, apparently becoming utterly shipwrecked as to her faith. To see this dear one, whom he thought of as one of the loveliest Christians he had ever known, pass out of Christian activity into oblivion, as it were, her mind beclouded with utterly false doctrines, was distressing beyond description to Captain Ironside.

Awakened, at last, the troubled young Christian (for he was now only in his nineteenth year) began to observe that this holiness teaching was leaving a tremendous train of spiritual derelicts. Not only his dear friend, nor just a few others, but scores of those who had come under the influence of this doctrine turned to what appeared to be downright infidelity. Their excuses were really one excuse, namely: "I tried it all, and it failed. The teaching of the Bible is a delusion and touches nothing but the emotions." Some of these lapsed into insanity later on. There was something wrong. The Scriptures declare, "God hath not given us the spirit of fear; but of power, and of love, and of a sound mind." It was not the study of the Bible that had driven these people crazy, as scoffers said, but it was lack of knowledge of the Bible that accounted for this wretched condition—of this Harry Ironside was sure.

Perplexed and distraught, Captain Ironside could not bear to go on any longer. After deliberating prayerfully over a period of many weeks, he sent in his resignation from the Salvation Army. It was not easy, for its evangelistic fervor had appealed to him from the beginning and generally he had been quite happy in this witness for Christ. Surely he had seen God working through his ministry of the Word. Harry's immediate superior begged him to reconsider his decision and to remain longer with the Army. The colonel even offered to send the captain on special missions where he would not need to come in contact with or hear holiness teaching. So Harry tried this for more than a month. But he felt himself falling a victim to despondency and began to wonder whether he, like some he had seen who claimed full sanctification but whose lives were nothing less than concealed hypocrisy, might be an out-and-out hypocrite whose heart God could see, even if others could not. He requested he be relieved of active service and sent to the Army's rest home in Oakland.

Completely worn out after five years of intensive work, during which he had taken only two brief furloughs, Captain Ironside entered the Beulah Rest Home, near Oakland, troubled in spirit and physically spent. Had he not gone there when he did, he might, within a few weeks, have experienced a total breakdown. For the first time in his life Harry welcomed the thought of rest. At the same time he looked forward to finding at Beulah what he had sought so long—"perfect sanctification." Surely in so sacred an atmosphere, he thought, the secret would no longer elude him!

Including Ironside there were fifteen officers there when he arrived, most of them broken in health, all of them seeking renewed strength that they might return to duty. The captain observed the ways and speech of these people, for it was his intention to seek out those who gave clearest evidence of complete holiness and to confide in them concerning his own lack of it. He found that the majority were really choice saints, although a few were unmitigated hyprocrites. Of holiness in the strictest and complete sense, he saw none. Yes, there were godly men and women there; but there is a difference between godliness and what was termed sinless perfection. There certainly was none of the latter. The most exemplary officers of all were three women. Two of them admitted that they themselves were not entirely sure about their own state of sanctification, while the third declined to commit herself.

There was a great deal of quarrelsomeness, jealousy, and positive boorishness at the home, and it was difficult for the unhappy captain to reconcile these things with profession of freedom from inbred sin. They seldom read the Bible and there was a significant lack of desire or even willingness to converse about the Person of the Lord Jesus Christ. Harry noticed that those who were the loudest talkers about "holiness" in meetings, were the least spiritual outside of the services, and his own disordered spirit, which he had hoped would be helped by the hallowed atmosphere of Beulah, was on the contrary hindered.

At the end of his first month at the home, Captain Ironside became practically an agnostic; for to every question based on divine revelation he was obliged to answer, "I do not know." His reasoning followed this vein: the Bible promises the elimination of indwelling sin from all who are completely surrendered to the will of God. Insofar as he himself could ascertain, he had surrendered wholly to God's will. But he had not been delivered from inbred sin. He was, he knew, carnal to the core. It appeared to him that he had met the condition required for sanctification but was not sanctified.

He had done his part; God had not done His part—or so it seemed. But that could not possibly be so! Harry had to confess he did not know the answer. After a while he refused even to think about it. He became cynical and cold to spiritual things. He stopped reading the Bible and sent for his secular books, which he had laid aside in "complete surrender" several years before. Upon their arrival, he sought solace in them rather than in the Word of God.

One day a lady who was said to be dying of tuberculosis arrived at the Beulah Home. She was a lieutenant in the Salvation Army. Her name was Alma Jungbeck and she was about thirty years of age. Harry's heart went out to her almost immediately, for she was a lovely character, and he looked upon her as a modern martyr who had indeed given her life for a needy world. From the time of her arrival he was much in her company and, as he watched her closely, he came to the conclusion that here at last was one who was unfeignedly and fully sanctified. What was his astonishment one evening when Lieutenant Jungbeck and another officer came to him and asked him to read to them! Miss Jungbeck said, "I hear that you are always occupied with the things of the Lord, and I need your help."

Imagine Ironside's bewilderment! Knowing the distress and doubts of his own heart, and having been assured of the holiness of hers, he was nonplused. He to help her? Why, it was she who should help him! As a matter of fact, at the moment that the two ladies had come to his door he had been reading Byron's *Childe Harold*—he who was supposed to be devoted to the things of the Lord! Utterly confused and embarrassed, he thrust aside his book, wondering all the while what he should read to his callers.

It was on impulse, an impulse assuredly directed by the Spirit of God, that Captain Ironside reached into a pile of papers for a tract his mother had given him several years before, one which he had never yet read. He had been so much a part of the Salvation Army that he had refrained from reading anything that did not bear its imprimatur or have the sanction of some holiness group, for he had feared that he might become confused by such writings. But now he felt impelled, and said to his callers, "I'll read this. It's not wholly in accord with our teaching, but it may be interesting at any rate."

Page after page he read, hoping more than anything else that the word would comfort the dying woman before him. The tract dealt with the lost condition of all men by nature and explained redemption through the shed blood of the Lord Jesus Christ. It told of the believer's two natures, and stressed what to its reader seemed absurd, that the believer in Christ was safe and secure eternally the moment he placed his trust in Him.

When he had finished reading, Harry was startled to hear Miss Jungbeck ask, "Captain, do you think that that can possibly be true? If I could only believe that, I could die in peace."

Amazed beyond measure, he exclaimed, "What! Do you mean to say that you could not die in peace as you are? You are justified and also sanctified. You have an experience that I've sought for years! Can you be troubled about dying?"

"I am miserable," Lieutenant Jungbeck replied.

"You must not say that I am sanctified. I can't get it. For years I've struggled but I've not reached it yet. That's why I came with my friend to speak to you tonight, for I've been so sure that you have it, and that you could help me."

For a moment they were both silent; then, affected at the same instant with the absurdity of the situation and despite its pathos, together they burst into almost delirious laughter and tears.

"Whatever is the matter with us all?" Harry asked. "No one on earth denies himself for Christ more than we in the Army do. We suffer, we almost starve, we wear ourselves out endeavoring to do the will of God. Yet with all this we have no lasting peace. We're happy at times. We enjoy our meetings. But we're never certain what the end will be."

"Do you think," was the prompt rejoinder, "that it is because we depend too much on our own efforts? Can it be that we trust Christ to save us but think that we must remain saved by our own faithfulness?"

"To think anything else," Ironside interrupted, "would open the door to all kinds of sin."

Far into the night they talked thus. Finally the two ladies, much wearied, excused themselves. It was mutually agreed to meet again that they might read and discuss further the things which had so stirred them.

That evening's exchange of confidences set Harry Ironside aflame to know the truth. Laying all his secular books aside, he began to search the Scriptures with vigor and in almost ceaseless prayer, determined to let nothing hinder his quest for light. In this search Lieutenant Jungbeck was hardly less zealous than he. Little by little the truth began to open to them. They found that they had been looking to the wrong person and wrong place for holiness—they had looked within themselves instead of outside of themselves. They began to comprehend that the same grace that saved them, and that alone, was the grace that could keep them.

With the light, however, came perplexity. Many things were difficult for Harry to understand, indoctrinated as he was with the teaching of holiness. It seemed to him now that so much that he had believed up to this time was absolutely contrary to God's Word. How could this be? So he got into communication with a businessman, who was also a Bible teacher and in fellowship with the writer of the pamphlet he had read on that momentous evening. This man, Charles Montgomery, opened up to him much truth, but the captain still felt confused, for he could not comprehend it all. Yet his feet were resting on solid ground, for he began to perceive that holiness, sanctification, perfect love, or whatever the term might be, belongs to the believer in Christ from the moment he believes, and that by God's grace and in Him it is his forever. A tract that is still well known and widely used, George Cutting's *Safety, Certainty, and Enjoyment,* was of tremendous help to both Captain Ironside and Lieutenant Jungbeck, as were other pamphlets. They read these with their Bibles in their hands and in prayer that God would open their eyes to His truth as written in His Word.

Alma Jungbeck saw the truth first, as she understood that she was eternally united with Christ as Head and had life eternal in Him, and that she was linked to Him as the branch is linked to the Vine—thus His life was hers also. Four days later the light likewise burst in upon Captain Ironside. He had been studying sanctification as it is taught in the Scriptures, to see that it means to be set apart. He saw that inanimate things could be sanctified, such as the altar (Exodus 40:10-11); people can sanctify themselves or others (Exodus 19:22; 13:2); the Father sanctified the Son, and the Son sanctified Himself (John 10:36; 17:19); carnal Christians can be sanctified (1 Corinthians 1:1-2; 3:1,3); and so also can unbelievers (1 Corinthians 7:14). He found moreover that those who are addressed as sanctified are later called upon to be holy (1 Peter 1:1-2,15-16), and that those who are called sanctified are said to be perfected forever (Hebrews 10:14). It came to him clearly that the holiness teaching that he had followed for so long was all wrong. There was no hint in these Scriptures of a change of the old nature in the believer in Christ, of the elimination of inbred sin, but rather that all Christians have received a new nature, are sanctified, separated to God in Christ, and that it is their responsibility to live for Him. Even in this responsibility He is their strength (Ephesians 6:10). Nothing is of self, except sin. All righteousness and perfection are in Christ.

When the blazing light of the truth pierced his soul, all doubts and fears were swept away. Liberty and joy reigned in his heart as he had never known them. He was free! He had found what he had been seeking—Christ was his "all, and in all."

PART 3

AMONG THE BRETHREN

"Because that for His name's sake they went forth,
taking nothing of the Gentiles."

3 JOHN 7

"In labours . . . By the word of truth,
by the power of God."

2 CORINTHIANS 6:5-7

8

A GOOD WIFE AND THE FAVOR
OF THE LORD

Within a week of the time when light concerning the headship of Christ entered his troubled soul and set him free from the despair he had endured for many months, Harry Ironside left the Salvation Army. The Army was the only human system he had ever known. Where was he to go? What should he do—return into secular work? The one business in which he could claim any experience was photography. Would Mr. Dando, the photographer whom he had left "to make a poor preacher," take him back? Perhaps he ought to spend some time at the Watsons' olive ranch in Monte Vista, where he was sure his mother and stepfather would welcome him. In his dilemma he sought out Charles Montgomery, who had helped him in his search for the truth about holiness teaching.

Mr. Montgomery owned two small hotels in San Francisco. He urged Harry to remain in the city for a while so that he might make the acquaintance of and have fellowship with a group of believers there whom Montgomery spoke of as the Brethren.* To make the

*Better known as Plymouth Brethren, these believers would prefer to be identified simply as brethren (with a small "b"). But because it is customary

way as easy as possible for the almost penniless young man, Montgomery provided living quarters for Harry in one of his hotels and offered him the freedom of his own splendid library. For a period of six months Ironside made his home there and reveled in writings that gave him fresh insight into the Bible.

Within two weeks he was asked to address the meeting where Montgomery and his friends gathered. Already he had recognized that these people knew the Scriptures well, and he wondered what to talk about. Once again he turned to Isaiah 53, that glorious chapter that had been his text on earlier signal occasions. God honored the Word that evening and, after the service, some of the brethren who had been told of his recent experiences and his uncertainty about the future, urged him to remain and teach the Word.

"But I know so little," Ironside told them. They encouraged him, however, to preach what he did know and to pursue his study of the Bible, telling him, "God will give you more as you go on."

Sooner than Charles Montgomery and some of the

for people to attach a label to almost every group or movement, in order also to avoid confusion with a denomination using the name Brethren, and in later years for recognition with the United States Government in the matter of chaplaincies, etc., these believers of whom Mr. Montgomery spoke accept, a bit reluctantly, the title Plymouth Brethren. The movement began in the nineteenth century in Dublin, Ireland, followed shortly thereafter by spontaneous meetings in Plymouth, Bristol, and London, England, the most active being in Plymouth.

The Church owes a great debt to the Brethren. Many of its early leaders, among them such devoted and gifted servants of Christ as J. G. Bellett, John Nelson Darby, William Kelly, C. H. Mackintosh, George Mueller, and Samuel Ridout, were the Holy Spirit's instruments to open up in a new way truths in the unchanging Scriptures. Through the spoken and written ministry of these and other men, there came to the Church a reemphasis of such important doctrines as the headship of Christ, the oneness of the body of Christ, the unity of the Spirit, and the imminent return of the Lord.

other brethren anticipated, Ironside was in demand as a speaker, not alone in San Francisco and its environs but far down the coast. Although he was remembered in a number of places for his evangelistic campaigns when he was a Salvation Army officer, Harry became impressed that he should minister to the saved as well as to the unsaved. Christians, he felt, needed to be stirred up to live more seriously in accordance with the truths they professed to hold. They needed, in fact, to learn what the Bible teaches and to abide by its precepts. Despite his amazing familiarity with the Bible as a whole, other than for his intensive search for the truth about justification and sanctification, he had not inquired a great deal into church truth as it is revealed in the Epistles, nor into many other deeper doctrines of God's Word. He was deluding neither himself nor others when he confessed to the brethren in San Francisco, "I know so little."

As a result he spent more and more time in poring over the Bible, comparing Scripture with Scripture. Occasionally, in his travels up and down California, Harry sought the communion and counsel of servants of God who were reported to know Christ intimately and to be well acquainted with the power of His resurrection and the fellowship of His sufferings. To this end, on one of his visits to Los Angeles he walked out far beyond the city limits to gain the acquaintance of an aged servant of the Lord who lived in a tent among the olive trees. His name was Andrew Fraser. He had been a friend of Sophia several years earlier but now, because he had contracted a contagious and terminal illness, he saw few people indeed. When Harry reached Mr. Fraser's tent and introduced himself, and after certain amenities were observed, the young man told his host that he was trying to preach the gospel and teach the Word.

"Well," said the aged servant of the Lord, "sit down for a while and let's talk together about the Word of God." He then opened his much-worn Bible and for some time, in fact, until his strength was about gone, earnestly presented truth after truth of the precious Word of God, turning from one passage to another. He did this in so simple and so sweet a manner that young Ironside entered into these truths in a way that he had never done before. Tears began running down the cheeks of the young preacher.

"Where did you get these things?" he asked. "Can you tell me where I can find a book that will open such wonderful truths to me? Did you learn these things in seminary?"

He waited for Mr. Fraser's answer, which he never forgot, "My dear young man, I learned these things on my knees on the mud floor of a little sod cottage in the north of Ireland. There with my open Bible before me I used to kneel for hours at a time and ask the Spirit of God to reveal Christ to my soul and to open the Word to my heart. He taught me more on my knees on that mud floor than I ever could have learned in all the colleges or seminaries in the world."

Ironside was anxious to get back to San Francisco, for he had fallen in love. Some months earlier, Henry Varley, a well-known British evangelist, had returned from a campaign in Australia by way of the United States. He spent three months in San Francisco to conduct a series of evangelistic services in the Metropolitan Temple there. Harry was enthusiastic about the campaign and spent many days helping in whatever way he could. He also ran a book table for Mr. Varley.

The pianist for most of these evening meetings was a former Salvation Army lassie, Captain Helen Schofield, daughter of a Presbyterian minister of Oakland. Harry was drawn to her immediately and in a matter of weeks considered asking her to marry him. He hesitated, however, for his financial situation was not at all what he thought it should be if he was to take a wife. Helen had been raised in a good home and he could not expect her to live by his faith. Here was his problem.

A distinctive mark in the practice of the Plymouth Brethren is that no man serves among them for a stated salary. They hold with the teaching of the Scriptures that every believer in Christ is a witness to Him, and they minister God's Word without prearranged remuneration but simply for Christ's sake. No assembly or meeting has an ordained minister in the sense in which that term is popularly understood today, for the Brethren hold that a man may have a God-given ministry without human ordination, including preaching ministry. It is their view that inasmuch as gifts have been bestowed by the Holy Spirit upon His people, every member of Christ's body is under obligation to fulfill whatever measure of the ministry has been committed to him. Those who teach or preach among the Brethren, therefore, receive no stipulated fee but are dependent completely upon the Lord for their support. The New Testament enjoins believers in Christ to lay aside on the first day of the week in accordance with the way the Lord prospers them. In such degree as an assembly of Christians is taught in the Word of God and abides by it, they will give to His work and share with those who are instruments of blessing to them. Harry understood this when he identified himself with the Brethren; so he lived and labored, trusting God to supply his needs from day to day. But did he have a right to ask Helen to do the same?

He who tells the Lord that he is going to trust Him will oftentimes be tested by Him. Harry did not forget the faithfulness of God to his mother in years gone by, and he was prepared to see the Lord work on his behalf. It was not long before he had an opportunity to watch the Lord do both—try him and work on his behalf.

Soon after his return to San Francisco from Los Angeles Harry began a series of meetings in one of the gospel halls of the city. It did not seem to occur to any of his listeners that he needed money, although he had so little that he came at length to his last five-cent piece. That day his sole food was a bag of peanuts. He had told the Lord of his need but, when evening came, still no one gave him anything. The next day he had no food at all, but again he preached three times. Another day passed in the same way and, when night fell, the young preacher wondered how he would have enough strength to get through the service. After his ninth message in three days without one bite of food, he overheard a maiden of uncertain age say: "I'm very much afraid that Mr. Ironside's love affair is hurting his soul. I don't think he preached with his usual power tonight." It was all he could do to resist hinting, "Try me on a beefsteak, sister!" But he said nothing and went home to bed, where he stayed also at breakfast time.

At ten o'clock in the morning a letter was delivered under his door. When he opened the envelope he found in it a ten-dollar bill, with no mention of the donor's name. But Harry knew who gave it to him—it was the Lord—and he thanked Him for it! It had been a time of testing. He had not broken down and asked for help. He had really trusted the Lord wholly. Ironside's spirit was encouraged and through the testing he grew in the knowledge of God's loving care.

The earnest young man told Helen of his recent experience. She agreed with him that profession of faith in God is not wholly genuine if he who professes it is not willing to trust God for everything.

"Do you really feel that way?" Harry inquired.

"Of course I do!" she replied.

Then Harry, who had been trying for what seemed like a very long time to discover the Lord's will for their lives, and aware also that "faint heart ne'er won fair lady," proposed marriage to Helen. Her answer was immediate, affirmative, and enthusiastic. Harry's lack of a nest egg was no obstacle to her who had been prepared, as a Salvationist, to suffer for Christ's sake. In fact, to the one as well as to the other, the most carefree life was a life of trust in God.

Ironside's love affair was not hurting his soul, despite what the gossiping spinster had suggested earlier. He continued to press forward in response to his heavenly calling, teaching and preaching whenever and wherever doors were opened to him. When no regular scheduled meeting called him, he would walk the streets of San Francisco and start a sidewalk service of his own, and soon have a fair audience.

One Sunday afternoon Mr. Ironside was walking along Market Street and noticed a sizable crowd gathered at the corner of Grant Avenue. He realized by the sound of the band and the singing that this was a Salvation Army meeting, and he joined the circle of people to enjoy the music and testimonies. The lassie captain knew him immediately, for it had hardly been more than a year since he left the Army. She asked him if he would like to give his testimony and he happily assented. While he was telling the gospel and of his own experience of God's saving grace, he observed a rather well-dressed and intelligent-looking man in the audience, standing a little apart from others. This gentlemen took a card out of his pocket and wrote something on it and, as Ironside was concluding his message, walked up to the "ring" and handed it to him.

Still speaking, Harry glanced down at the card and promptly recognized the name of a man who had been giving widely-advertised addresses on the West Coast for some months. He was an official representative of one of the early trade unions, the I.W.W.—the Industrial Workers of the World, facetiously called by its opponents, I Won't Work. This particular man was famed for his ability to incite his hearers to class hatred and animosity toward the capitalistic system. He had passed him the card, Harry realized, for a purpose other than to give him his name, so Harry turned it over and read the penciled words, "Sir, I challenge you to debate with me the question 'Agnosticism vs. Christianity' in the Academy of Science Hall next Sunday afternoon at four o'clock. I will pay all expenses."

Harry read the card aloud to the crowd; he then answered his challenger, "I'm very much interested in this challenge. Frankly, I've already been announced as the speaker at another meeting next Lord's day afternoon at three o'clock, but I think it will be possible to finish in time to reach the Academy of Science by four or, if necessary, to have another speaker take my place at the earlier meeting.

"Therefore," he continued, "I'll be glad to agree to this debate on the following conditions, namely that in order to prove that this gentleman has something worth debating about, he will promise to bring with him to the hall next Sunday two people whose qualifications I shall give in a moment, as proof that agnosticism is of real value in changing human lives and building true character. First, he must promise to bring with him one man who was for years what we commonly call a 'down-and-outer.' I'm not particular as to the exact nature of the sins that wrecked his life and made him an outcast from society—whether he was a drunkard, or a criminal of some kind, or a victim of any sensual appetite. He must be, however, a man who for years was under the power of some evil habits from which he could not deliver himself, but who, on some occasion, attended one of this gentleman's meetings and heard him speak, glorifying agnosticism and denouncing the Bible and Christianity, and whose heart and mind as he listened to such an address were so deeply stirred that he went away from that meeting saying, 'Henceforth I, too, am an agnostic!' or words to that effect, and as a result of embracing that particular philosophy he found that a new power had come into his life. The sins that he once loved, now he hates, and righteousness and goodness are henceforth the ideals of his life. He is now an entirely new man, a credit to himself and an asset to society—all because he is an agnostic.

"Secondly," Ironside went on to say, "I would like this gentleman who has challenged me to debate to bring with him to the hall next Sunday one woman— and I think he may have more difficulty in finding the woman than the man—who was once a poor, wretched, characterless outcast, the slave of degrading passions and the victim of man's corrupt living. Perhaps," said, Harry, nodding in the direction of San Francisco's in-famous Barbary Coast, which was only a stone's throw from the spot where he was speaking, "perhaps one who had lived for years in some notorious resort down there on Pacific Street, or in some other hell-hole, ut-terly lost, ruined, and wretched. But this woman also entered one of this gentleman's meetings and heard him loudly proclaiming his agnosticism and ridiculing the message of the Holy Scriptures. As she listened to him, hope was born in her heart and she said, 'This is just what I need to deliver me from the slavery of sin!' She followed this teaching, then, until she became an intelligent agnostic or infidel. As a result, her whole being revolted against the degradation of the life she had been living. She fled from the infamous place where she had been captive so long and today, rehabilitated, she has won her way back to an honored position in society and is living a clean, virtuous, happy life—all because she is an agnostic.

"Now, sir," Harry continued, "if you will promise to bring with you two such people as examples of what agnosticism will do, I will promise to meet you at the Academy of Science Hall at the hour appointed next Sunday, and I'll bring with me at the very least one hundred men and women who for years lived in just such sinful degradation as I have tried to depict but who have been gloriously saved through believing the message of the gospel which you ridicule. I'll have these men and women with me on the platform as witnesses to the miraculous saving power of Jesus Christ, and as present-day proof of the truth of the Bible."

Quickly turning to the Salvation Army captain, Ironside asked, "Captain, have you any who could go with me to such a meeting?"

"We can give you forty, at least," she exclaimed enthusiastically, "all from this one corps, and we'll furnish a brass band to lead the procession."

"Fine!" Harry said, "Now, sir," facing his challenger, "I shall have no difficulty in picking up at least sixty others from various missions, gospel halls, and evangelical churches. So if you promise faithfully to bring two such 'exhibits' as I have described, I will come marching in at the head of such a procession, with the band playing Onward Christian Soldiers, and I'll be ready for the debate."

His opponent, who had at least some sense of humor, smiled rather sardonically and, with a wave of the hand as if to say, "Nothing doing!" walked away from the scene of the meeting—while the crowd applauded and cheered the street preacher who had met the challenge of the agnostic and put him to flight. They recognized immediately that no philosophy of negation, such as agnosticism, could ever make bad men and women good, and yet they knew from observation and experience that this is exactly what Christ has done for centuries and is doing every day.

Mr. Ironside continued thus to witness to Christ in and out of season—and the months rolled by. Late in the year God answered his prayers, the Spirit seeming to seal the troth of Harry and his loved one when he received a legacy of three hundred dollars from the estate of his grandfather in Scotland. It was not a fortune but more than Harry had ever had at one time in his life. If the eager young man needed any "fleece," this was it. Certainly it was the prayed-for nest egg.

So at the turn of the year, on January 5, 1898, Henry Allan Ironside and Helen Georgia Schofield were married.

9

I HAVE COMMANDED THE RAVENS
TO FEED THEE

The young couple, Mr. and Mrs. Henry Allan Ironside, took a year's lease on an apartment in San Francisco even though they knew that they would have to be on the road a great deal of the time. They needed a place for their furniture and other possessions, and Harry's expanding library required space too.

There was one occasion of testing when they were in Sacramento for a month, living in a house supplied them by the Brethren group to whom Harry was ministering. Mrs. Schofield, Helen's mother, visited them unexpectedly. Funds were quite low; in fact the only food in the house was a sack of beans. The day Mrs. Schofield arrived Helen served beans for luncheon and beans again for supper. The next morning the breakfast fare was the same. When beans composed the menu for lunch the second day Mrs. Schofield, who had been silent to this time concerning the peculiar diet, could hold her tongue no longer.

"Helen," she exclaimed, "you two are the greatest hands for beans I've ever seen in my life! I didn't bring you up this way."

Without so much as raising an eyebrow Helen

answered, "Well, Mama, Harry is *so* fond of beans."

"It's all right to be fond of them," Mrs. Schofield said, "but surely you don't want them all the time."

Harry got up from the table and went to his room, where he knelt down and implored the Lord to break the monotony. Later in the afternoon, as he was walking to the post office, he met an old Scotsman who had been attending the evening services at the gospel hall. He handed Harry a dollar. The young preacher lost his "fondness" for beans in a hurry and, finding a butcher shop, bought some provisions. A dollar went a long way in 1898, and the family of three had a banquet that evening.

Again and again the Ironsides were called upon to exercise faith in God for their daily needs. They considered these experiences testing times. If Harry was to preach concerning the Lord's loving care of His people, he must experience for himself and Helen a trusting spirit under trying circumstances. How can a believer ever be thought worthy to rule in many things, he used to ask himself, unless he has proved himself faithful in a few things?

Nevertheless there were times when Harry became extremely despondent; but only once did he seriously consider leaving full-time ministry in the Lord's service for secular employment. The young couple had been without food for two days. Despite their plight Helen, whose faith never wavered at any time, prayed that her husband's faith would not fail under this trial, that he would not turn aside from what both of them had agreed was God's purpose for his life—to preach the gospel without charge to anyone, waiting contentedly for whatever might come to him from the hand of God. That very afternoon Harry received a five-dollar gold piece provided by his heavenly Father through a friend. The Lord knew that this was the precise hour to meet the need of His faithful if faltering servant.

Late that same year, while the Ironsides were still in Sacramento, word came that Harry's mother was very ill. They felt that they must leave immediately for Long Beach, where the Watsons were then living, not only to nurse Sophia through her sickness but also to assist her by taking care of Lillian, four-year-old daughter of the Watsons. Within a few days after the young couple's arrival at the Watson home, Harry's mother was taken into the presence of Christ. This was a period of deep trial in many ways for Harry and Helen. No ties were left, it seemed, in the little family that had come from Ontario to California, for Harry's brother John was then living in the Philippines. And then, only a few months later, Helen's father died.

As sunshine follows rain, so rejoicing succeeded sorrow in the Ironside family. On February 10, 1899, in the city of Los Angeles, a son was born to the Ironsides—Edmund Henry. Harry moved Helen and the baby from the apartment in San Francisco to a house in Oakland. They took Lillian, now five, with them (she was, after all, Harry's half sister), for her father could not care for her properly, since his work now took him to various cities in the midwest. In due course and with her father's consent, the Daniel McFies, old friends of Watson and childless, brought Lillian into their home and raised her as though she were their own daughter.

From time to time Ironside used to mail some Christian literature to Brethren assemblies and local churches. A gentleman in Fresno who had received encouragement from some of these tracts, wrote Harry and asked him to come to Fresno when circumstances would permit. The correspondent said that he would arrange a number of Bible-teaching meetings for Harry and that the latter could stay in his home while he was there.

Months passed before Ironside had any reason to go to Fresno. But at length he had some engagements in East Bakersfield and, when they were about fulfilled, he got a distinct impression that he should stop off at Fresno on his way back to Oakland. He was somewhat puzzled about this. The Holy Spirit generally speaks to the Lord's servants through the Word, not by impressions; but Harry's inward feelings concerning a visit to Fresno were so unusual and persistent that he decided to go there. He gave all his money, excepting one dollar, to Helen and took the train northward. When he stepped off the train at Fresno he left his bag at the station and found his way to the house of his intended host. What was his dismay when he discovered the house closed up! Neighbors informed him that the family would be away some weeks. It seemed a clear rebuke from the Lord, a reprimand to show him not to follow impressions, however strong they might be.

Well, there he was in Fresno and without sufficient money to get home. He went back to the station, recovered his suitcase and looked for inexpensive lodging. He found a room at twenty-five cents a night. It was evening. In his room he bowed his knees, asking God to show him if he had erred and to reveal the next step to him. Perhaps He would give him some indication where he might minister in the city. While he was still praying he heard singing in the street, so he went out. A Salvation Army meeting was in progress. Harry listened for a short time, but when the collection was being taken he departed, feeling that his circumstances hardly permitted his having a share in it. At the very next corner he came across another street meeting, this one under the direction of the Peniel Mission of Los Angeles. The testimonies and the Word as it was given had a good evangelical sound, so he decided to go to their hall, where a service was to be held. When Harry got there the place was nearly filled and he slipped quietly into a seat in the rear and near the door. Glancing at the platform, he was conscious of the fact that two ladies who were seated there, apparently to lead the meeting, were staring at him and whispering about him. That he was noticed immediately on his arrival was not astonishing, for Harry had grown a beard and it was very red. Nonetheless he was rather embarrassed to be the subject of discussion. In a moment, one of the women left the platform and walked directly to him.

"Are you the one who is to preach here tonight?"

"I don't know," Harry answered.

"Aren't you a preacher of the gospel?" she inquired.

"Yes, I am."

"And haven't you a message for us tonight?"

"I'm not sure," Harry replied. "Why do you ask?"

"This other lady and I have charge of the meeting tonight," she answered. "We were praying today about this evening and it seemed to both of us as though a voice spoke, saying, 'I shall send My own messenger tonight. You will know him when you see him.' And so," she continued, "we were watching every one who entered the door, and when you came in we felt sure that you were God's messenger."

Fitting as it did with his own experience, Ironside, who as a rule did not give credence to such a "voice," accepted it as an opening from God and told the lady how he happened to be in Fresno.

"Then you must be the Lord's messenger," was her answer. "Please come to the platform."

After the service, some expressed gratitude for the message and the two ladies asked the young man to remain for two weeks, holding meetings every night, as well as on the Lord's day in the afternoon and evening.

This first service was on a Friday night. No one had asked Harry whether he had accommodations and, since he was looking to God to supply his needs, he dared not mention them to others unless they first asked about them. So he stayed that night and the next day at his lodging house, eating very sparingly indeed. Late Saturday afternoon, therefore, absolutely penniless and having had only five-cents' worth of food all day, he took his suitcase from the room he had been using and asked permission of a druggist to leave his baggage in his store. That evening Harry felt terribly alone and rather discouraged. No food, no lodging— and then his heart lifted as he recalled Another who said, "The foxes have holes, and the birds of the air have nests; but the Son of man hath not where to lay His head."

Harry usually carried with him a large quantity of gospel tracts. After preaching that night he crossed over into the very worst part of the city, where saloons, dance halls, and gambling houses were in abundance, and visited one after another of these places, giving out tracts and bearing personal testimony when he could find a ready ear. At length all the leaflets, almost 3,000 of them, were disposed of. It was two o'clock in the morning and even the saloons were closing. Not having a place to go, Harry began walking along the trolley tracks and out into the suburbs to the end of the line, where he laid down on a bench in an empty trolley car and tried to sleep. It was a cold night. He could neither keep warm nor make himself comfortable. He tried to pray but seemed unable to do so. He was hardly in the spirit of prayer, for he was complaining to God, on whose promise of Philippians 4:19 he had counted. I have a need, he said to himself, but God has not supplied it. I have been seeking with all my strength to serve Him, and He has failed me. Perplexed and out of sorts, since he could not sleep, he got up at about four o'clock and walked back into the center of the city.

In the grounds of the courthouse he saw a large weeping willow, whose branches hung low on all sides. He crawled under them and managed to sleep for a couple of hours near its trunk. When he wakened it seemed that God was speaking very clearly to him in regard to certain things about which he had allowed himself to become careless. Under the leafy bower of the willow he poured out his heart to Him, confessing his lack of faith, his self-will, and other things that were brought to his remembrance by the Holy Spirit. As the list of errors and failures enlarged he no longer wondered that when he called upon the Lord there had seemed to be no answer; and then he began to praise the Lord for all that He had done and for His unfailing mercies. Refreshed by this hour with the Lord, Harry went over to the fountain by the courthouse, washed his hands and his face, and set off toward the Methodist Church, where he had been invited to teach a class of young men.

Presiding at the opening exercise of the Sunday school was a man who had been Harry's Sunday school teacher a few years earlier in Los Angeles, who, when Harry made himself known, was overjoyed to see him and took him to a fine dinner after the church services. In the afternoon Harry spoke at Peniel Hall. Following the meeting a young osteopath, who had been helped by the Word, introduced himself and asked, "At what hotel are you staying?"

"I have been staying in such-and-such a section," Harry said, mentioning the area but no hotel.

"Could you come and stay with me?" the doctor inquired. "I live alone in an apartment where I have a spare room. I get lonesome for Christian fellowship and would be delighted to have you with me as long as you remain in Fresno."

Harry assented eagerly. His friend offered, then, to walk with him to his hotel for his bag, but Harry, thinking of the drugstore, assured him that that would be unnecessary. So he went alone and before long joined his host in his comfortable apartment.

While supper was being prepared the doctor, observing Harry's weariness, proposed that he take a nap. The latter, who could hardly keep his eyes open, was only too glad to follow the suggestion. The next thing he knew he was dreaming that he was passing through a most fearful earthquake—only to discover that it was his host trying to rouse him for supper.

Mr. and
Mrs.
Ironside
with
Edmund
1902

H. A. Ironside
at the Beginning
of His Writing
Ministry

"My, Brother Ironside," he exclaimed, "you certainly are a sound sleeper!"

At the evening service, fortified with two excellent meals and an hour's sleep, and his heart filled with praise to God for His goodness, the young preacher seemed to have unusual liberty and God wrought in great power. Several confessed Christ as Lord and Saviour at the meeting's end. Afterward, one after another came to shake Harry's hand, at the same time slipping money into his palm. When he returned to his friend's apartment he counted what the Lord had sent him. It was more than twenty-seven dollars! On Monday morning Harry sent a good part of the sum to his wife in Oakland, retaining only sufficient to provide for him through the series of meetings and pay his carfare home.

When he went to the post office the next day, Harry inquired for mail and was handed a letter from his step-father, William Watson. Taking the letter from its envelope, his eyes fell immediately upon a postscript under Watson's signature. This is what it said:

"God spoke to me through Philippians 4:19 today. He has promised to supply all our need. Some day He may see that I need a starving. If He does, He will supply that."

It should not be thought that the Ironsides were always on a starvation diet or that every day of their lives was marked by a miraculous last-minute provision from God's hand. Of course God took care of them. Of course they trusted Him to supply their needs. And of course there were long periods when nothing unusual occurred, when life went on day by day in much the same way it does with most of us. Yet there were experiences still to be borne when Harry's faith would waver, as in 1903 when a group of believers in Minnesota sent Ironside his first invitation from the east.

The ministry in St. Cloud ended after two weeks and Harry took Helen and Edmund, who had accompanied him to Minnesota, to visit several other Brethren assemblies in that general area. They planned to go directly home from Chicago but had only sufficient money for railway fare as far as Salt Lake City. So to Salt Lake City they went, where Harry obtained accommodations in an inexpensive hotel. He felt that, under the circumstances, the Lord must surely have a ministry for him there. For ten days he spent every afternoon and evening distributing tracts from door to door, and some evenings he preached the gospel at a street corner. But no one seemed interested in his message or in fellowship of any kind. As his testimony was seemingly rejected and his funds began to dwindle, his faith dwindled. He became somewhat disgruntled that God should treat him this way, for he was at the end of the rope. The three of them were subsisting on forty cents a day for their meals, the hotel bill was due, and there was no money to pay it.

Greatly troubled in spirit, Harry went for a long walk in the snow, for it was winter. He began thinking about the promises of God, reciting them one by one over and over again. Nothing seemed to help him. He would quote our Lord's covenant, "If ye abide in Me, and My words abide in you, ye shall ask what ye will, and it shall be done unto you." But, he thought, how can that help me? I am not abiding in the Lord, so it is futile to ask. Then another Scripture text would come to his mind, "Whatsoever ye shall ask in prayer, believing, ye shall receive"—but this promise seemed to defy him, for his faith was gone and he could not pray believingly. Another and another promise of provision crossed his thoughts, "Be anxious for nothing"—but he *was* anxious; "My God shall supply all your need"—but he *had* a need, and it had not been supplied; "My grace is sufficient for thee"—but *grace* would not satisfy Edmund's hunger. Then there flashed before his memory as if on a screen, "If two of you shall agree on earth as touching any thing that they shall ask, it shall be done for them of My Father who is in heaven."

Without waiting to analyze the verse, not aware that the word "agree" has to do with being in harmony with God as well as with each other, he took hold of this promise and rushed back to the hotel. Helen too was distressed over their circumstances and readily joined her husband in prayer, the two "agreeing" as to their need. Harry asked God that that very night He would provide forty cents so that they might have food for the next day. He remembered the rest of his life his distraught and rather pitiable prayer, which he concluded thus: "O Lord, we claim this promise. We two are agreed to ask for this forty cents. If we do not receive it, I shall never believe this verse again." Helen protested. How could he speak to God in such a fashion? But he was adamant: that was how he felt, and that was how he must pray. He went out into the street again to preach the gospel to whomever he could, reiterating to Helen, "This is the test. If God does not hear us, I simply cannot pray any more."

Finding a likely corner, Harry preached, though he himself wondered how he could do it. For forty minutes he addressed a crowd of about three hundred. When he had finished and turned to go home, he felt sure that someone would offer an expression of thanks in some material form, but none did. In bitterness of soul he was going his way when he noticed two men hurrying after him. He stopped.

One of the men said, "You forgot something, didn't you?"

"What was that?"

"You forgot to take a collection."

"I never take them in my own meetings," Harry said.

"Well, how do you live then?" he was asked.

"Why," the preacher answered, "I just trust the Lord and He meets my needs." Even as he spoke he realized that it was hypocrisy to answer in this way. How could he say he was trusting the Lord when he was doing no such thing?

But one of the men was speaking, "Well, shake hands anyway," and reaching out his hand he took Harry's, who felt several coins in his palm. The other man shook Harry's hand in the same manner.

Ironside started to thank them and then realized that he did not know them. Perhaps they were not Christians! It was not his custom to accept anything from the "Gentiles," the unsaved, for he believed that God's work will be supported by God through His people.

"Gentlemen," he said, "I do thank you. But are you Christians yourselves? I do not accept money from the unsaved."

"That's all right," one of them said, "we know all about it. We've been out for two years without scrip or purse ourselves."

Harry knew then that they were Mormon elders. He

was about to insist that he must return their gifts, but they hurried away and were soon lost in the crowd. Harry opened his hand then, to find two dimes and four nickles—exactly forty cents! God does not always work in the way we expect Him to, and this time, to supply the need of His servant who had prayed in such a complaining way, whose faith had been so small, He sent two ravens, men of an alien faith, to grant his exact request.

The next day a letter that had been forwarded from Oakland came in the morning mail. It was a joint message from two earnest believers and read as follows: "We were praying for you last night. We do not know where you are, but we feel impressed that you need money. We have put our gifts together and enclose a check for fifteen dollars."

God had not forgotten His ill-tempered and wavering servant even when the latter had been in such a distraught and faithless state of mind. Before he had even asked, the answer had been on its way, "exceeding abundantly above all" that he had asked or thought. "It is of the LORD'S mercies that we are not consumed, because His compassions fail not. They are new every morning: great is Thy faithfulness."

10

AN HOLY PRIESTHOOD

It may be recalled that when Harry Ironside left the Salvation Army and became acquainted with the Plymouth Brethren in San Francisco, some of the brethren urged him to remain there and teach the Word of God. When he told them he was reluctant to do so because, as he said, "I know so little," their response was, "God will give you more as you go on." From that time onward there was a notable augmentation to Harry's preaching of the gospel, for now he was careful to impress upon his audiences the background and context of his sermon topics.

Still conscious of his limited formal education, Harry filled this lack with an awesome reading schedule. He devoured every worthwhile piece of literature he could lay his hands on, so as to enlarge his usefulness as a servant of the Lord. The writings of Roman Catholic church fathers and theologians, and of sectarian authors like Gibbon and Newman, were almost as familiar to him as those of the Puritan writers and of Darby, Kelly, Hodge, and others of the nineteenth century. Having at his command an incredibly retentive memory, his reading in these early years proved invaluable throughout his life. Reading never tired his mind but stimulated it, and his frequent travel by railroad gave him an additional opportunity to cultivate knowledge.*

The worth of this self-education may be illustrated by an incident that took place in 1904. Harry, Helen and little Edmund were on an all-day train trip in a province in northwestern Canada.** Shortly after they boarded the train in the early morning it stopped at a wayside station, where a Franciscan priest, wearing the customary brown frock of that order, got aboard and entered the car where the Ironside family was occupying double seats facing each other. The car was crowded and the monk seated himself on a woodbox situated at the rear. (Passenger cars were heated by wood-burning stoves in those days.)

Solicitous for a fellow traveler's comfort and sensing, too, an opportunity to witness of Christ to the priest, Harry suggested to his wife that they rearrange their baggage. Then he went back and invited the stranger to share the seats which he and his little family were occupying. The priest accepted the invitation with gratitude and pleasure.

After the Franciscan sat down he and Ironside entered into conversation such as is usually introduced in such circumstances, discussing the weather, the terrain, world conditions, crops, and the like. At length, however, the monk gave Harry the opportunity for

---

*For H. A. Ironside's own remarks about books that helped him most, see Appendix C.

** This was, in fact, Helen's last long speaking tour with Harry for some time. The next summer, on August 18, 1905, a second son, John Schofield, was born to the Ironsides and from then on Helen was too busy raising the two boys to be able to accompany her husband regularly.

which he had been watching, as he inquired as to where the Ironsides lived and what Harry's business was. Harry told him that in some respects they were both engaged in the same kind of work, adding that he, like the Franciscan, was a catholic priest employed in missionary ministry.* The monk glanced at Harry's wife and child, then at his collar, and said, "You are jesting, I think."

Harry assured his companion that he was indeed a catholic priest but not a Roman Catholic priest. "You will pardon me," he remarked, "if I say that to my mind 'Roman' and 'Catholic' do not fit well together. The former suggests a restricted communion, whereas the latter speaks of a universal church."

"You mean, then, you are an Anglican clergyman?"

"No," Ironside replied, "I do not consider myself a clergyman, nor am I an Anglican. 'Anglican,' too, suggests restriction. I am, as I told you, a priest in the holy catholic Church instituted by our Lord Jesus Christ Himself. Perhaps it would make things clearer if I gave you some account of how I became a Christian, and how I was made a priest."

The Franciscan assured Ironside that he would be most interested in hearing of this. Then Harry narrated the story of his conversion at the age of fourteen, somewhat as it has been recorded in an earlier chapter, stressing the point that it was through reading the Word of God, namely Romans 3 and John 3,

---

*In 1938 I shared a Bible conference platform with Dr. Ironside. He told the story of his conversation with a Franciscan monk aboard a train in Canada. I urged him to let me have it in writing for *Revelation* magazine, of which I was then managing editor. He did so. It was published in *Revelation* and in 1939 was included in a book by Ironside entitled *Random Reminiscences,* published by Loizeaux Brothers, Inc.

that the light of salvation in Christ broke upon his soul. When told how he had cried out then, "Lord, I do believe, and I dare to trust Thy Word. I am not condemned"—the monk, who had been listening very intently, broke out with an exclamation.*

"That is most interesting!" he ejaculated. "I have never heard anything like it in my life. You remind me of St. Augustine."

I was a bit amused and puzzled, and I tried to think in what way my simple story would put him in mind of the great doctor of Hippo. "I do not quite understand," I said, "why you compare me to him."

"Well," he answered, "do you not remember it was through the Book that the light came to him, without any individual's speaking to him? And so with you—the light came through the Book!"

"Ah," I replied, "I do get the connection perfectly. It was indeed through the Word of God itself that I was led into light and peace and the full assurance of salvation."

"But now," asked the priest, "what did you do next? Augustine, after he became a Christian, went to a priest for further instruction, and finally became a great doctor of the church."

"Well," I replied, "I sought out a little group of Christians with whom I soon had happy fellowship, and continued studying my Bible. It was as I studied the First Epistle of the Apostle Peter that I made a very great discovery. I found out that I was not only a child of God, the possessor of eternal life, but that the moment I was saved I became a priest in the holy catholic Church. The apostle tells us in the second chapter, verse 5, 'Ye also, as living stones, are built up a spiritual house, an holy priesthood, to offer up spiritual sacrifices, acceptable to God by Jesus Christ'; and in verse nine he says, 'But ye are a chosen generation, a royal priesthood, an holy nation, a peculiar people; that ye should show forth the praises of Him who hath called you out of darkness into His marvelous light.'

"From these Scriptures I learned," I went on to say, "that I am a priest, set apart in Christ Jesus as a worshiper, and that it is my blessed privilege to be Christ's representative in this world, seeking to make known the riches of His grace to others."

---

*From here to its conclusion the story is told in the words of Ironside, as written in *Random Reminiscences.*

Smiling, the Franciscan said, "I understand now what you meant by saying that you are a catholic priest. But you are not a member of the true church which Jesus Christ founded on St. Peter."

This led to a long though friendly discussion as to the nature of the true Church, and also as to Peter's relation to it, and from this we went on to talk of the new birth, the sacraments—particularly the real nature of the Lord's Supper and the purpose for which it was given—and such themes as purgatory, prayers to the saints, the relative place of faith and good works, and other subjects. In a friendly way we discussed the many other topics concerning which Romanists and Protestants differ. The Franciscan confessed frankly that he was at a loss in keeping up his side in such a discussion because of the fact that he was, he regretted to say, not familiar with the Bible. He told me that his studies had largely occupied him with the writings of the church fathers and the decrees of the church, and that he realized that he had not read the Holy Scriptures as carefully as he should have done. I thought I could detect a yearning for something deeper than he had ever known, as he opened up his heart along certain lines which I do not feel free to commit to print.

He shared our lunch with us, and was most gracious and friendly throughout the whole day. As evening drew on, our train pulled into the station of the city where I was to preach that night. A relative of mine, at whose home we were to be entertained, was waiting for us, and was a bit surprised when we two "priests" descended the steps of the car together. My cousin took charge of my wife and little boy, while the "priests" walked on ahead conversing all the way about the great truths that have to do with our salvation.

Finally we reached the corner where our ways must part—he to go to the right to the monastery, and I to the left to my cousin's home. He became more and more interested and, as we were about to separate, said, "I wish you could come up to the monastery and spend the evening with me! I cannot ask the lady to come, as it is contrary to our rules, but if you could possibly spare the evening I would be so glad to talk with you further, and I would have an opportunity there of showing you just what the fathers have said. We could consult many books in the library, which I think might help to make some of my points clear to you."

I assured him that I would enjoy spending such an evening, but a dinner appointment at my cousin's home and a preaching engagement later would make that impossible. I suggested that he come with us, as I knew my relatives would gladly welcome him, and then he could go to the service with us.

To this he demurred, saying that it would not do for him to attend a Protestant conventicle in his ecclesiastical garb, as it might give rise to misunderstandings.

Somewhat mischievously I said, "Well, you and I are of about the same build, and in my bag here I have another suit. If you will come down to dinner with us I will give you an opportunity to dress up like a man, in my clothes, and no one will know the difference!"

He laughed at this and said, "Ah, but I have taken a solemn vow always to wear this attire."

"In that case," I replied, "I would not for a moment seek to have you break your vow."

He took my hand very earnestly and said, "I suppose we will have to part. I cannot tell you how I have enjoyed this day with you! It is the first time I have ever talked these things over with a Protestant clergyman who did not get angry with me."

"But I *will* be angry with you," I told him, "if you do not accept the statement which I have made concerning myself. I am not a clergyman but a priest of the catholic Church."

"Ah, yes," he said, "I had forgotten! But let me say again how greatly I have enjoyed the day. I shall often think of you, and I hope you will pray for me—as I for you. I do not suppose we shall ever meet again, but I shall not forget the things that we have talked about."

"We shall indeed meet again, and that on one of two occasions," I told him.

"Ah, you mean either in Heaven or in hell!"

"No, I do not mean that at all. If you go to hell, which I trust will never be the case, I certainly will not meet you there, for I have been washed from my sins in the precious blood of Christ and I know that I shall be with Him in Heaven through all eternity."

"What, then, do you mean by 'one of two occasions'?"

"Well, perhaps very soon now, 1 Thessalonians 4.15-17 will be fulfilled. I hope I shall meet you then."

"1 Thessalonians 4:15-17," he repeatedly slowly, as though trying to charge his mind with the passage. "I regret to say that I am not familiar enough with the Epistle to know what passage you refer to."

I quoted the words, " 'For this we say unto you by the word of the Lord, that we who are alive and remain unto the coming of the Lord, shall not precede them which are asleep. For the Lord Himself shall descend from Heaven with a shout, with the voice of the archangel, and with the trump of God; and the dead in Christ shall rise first: then we who are alive and remain shall be caught up together with them in the clouds, to meet the Lord in the air; and so shall we ever be with the Lord.'

"We are not told when this event will take place," I added, "but if I understand the Scriptures aright, it might come at any moment. When this Scripture is fulfilled and the Lord descends from Heaven, all who are trusting in Him, and in Him alone, as their Saviour, will be caught up to meet Him. The dead will be raised, and the living changed. I shall be among that number, although an unworthy sinner in myself; for the precious blood of Christ has cleansed me and made me meet to be a partaker of the inheritance of the saints in light."

"You must feel that you are a very good man," he broke in, "to be so sure that you will be there!"

"No, it is not that at all. I found out years ago, as I have told you, that I am anything but good. I learned from the Word of God that my heart was 'deceitful above all things and desperately wicked.' I saw that I was a lost sinner, and I fled to Christ for refuge. And I saw that all who trust in Him are justified from all things. When this great event to which this Scripture refers takes place and all believers are caught up to meet the Lord, I shall look for you, and if your faith and confidence have been—not in the church, not in sacraments, not in your merits, your prayers, or your good works—but in the Lord Jesus Christ alone, who died on Calvary to settle the sin question, I shall meet you there, and we shall have a wonderful time together rejoicing in the fullness of God's salvation."

He looked at me inquiringly for a moment, and then in a subdued voice he said, "You spoke of 'two occasions.' What was the other that you had in mind?"

"Well," I replied, "if I do not see you in the air when the Lord Jesus comes, I won't look for you for a thousand years."

"A thousand years! Why do you say 'a thousand years'?"

"Because another Scripture text says, 'Blessed and holy is he that hath part in the first resurrection: on such the second death hath no power, but they shall be priests of God and of Christ, and shall reign with Him a thousand years.' The preceding verse says, 'But the rest of the dead lived not again until the thousand years were finished.' And after the expiration of that thousand years, John says, 'And I saw a great white throne, and Him that sat on it, from whose face the earth and the heaven fled away; and there was found no place for them.   And I saw the dead, small and great, stand before God; and the books were opened: and another book was opened, which is the book of life; and the dead were judged out of those things which were written in the books, according to their works. And the sea gave up the dead which were in it; and death and hell delivered up the dead which were in them; and they were judged every man according to their works. And death and hell were cast into the lake of fire. This is the second death. And whosoever was not found written in the book of life was cast into the lake of fire.'

"When that stupendous event, the last great assize, takes place," I told him, "I shall be there with the Lord. But I shall not stand in front of that great white throne to be judged, for all my judgment passed when those two arms were outstretched on Calvary, when, as a poet has said:

The wrath of God which was our due
Upon the Lamb was laid,
And by the shedding of His blood
Our debt was fully paid.

"Christ has said, as you have it in your Roman Catholic version of the Scriptures, in John 5:24, 'Amen, Amen, I say to you, he who hears My Word, and believes Him who sent Me, has eternal life, and comes not into judgment, but is passed out of death into life.' But though I shall not come into judgment for my sins, I shall be with Christ in that day, for we are told that the saints shall judge the world, and shall even judge angels! And if I have not found you among the redeemed at the Lord's return, I shall look over that vast sea of faces which will come from all the graveyards of the earth and from the depths of the sea; and if you have lived and died trusting for your salvation in the church and in its sacraments, in your prayers, your charity, or your good deeds, I will see you there—a poor lost soul; and I will see the awful look that will come over your face as the blessed Lord shall say to you, 'Depart from Me, ye cursed, into everlasting fire prepared for the devil and his angels!' "

"God forbid! God forbid!" he fairly cried aloud. He was trembling in his excitement.

I put my hand upon his shoulder tenderly. "Yes, God forbid!—for in order that it might not be, Jesus died! He died for you—He, the sinless One, was made sin for you that you might become the righteousness of God in Him. Tell me, is it Christ or the church? Is it His blood, or is it your own merits? In which do you trust?"

He was silent a moment or two. Then, looking up with tear-dimmed eyes, he exclaimed, "Oh, Christ! *He* is the Rock! Christ— He is the Rock! I dare not trust in anyone but Him. I trust my soul to Him alone!"

"Give me your hand, my brother," I exclaimed. "For now you, too, speak like Augustine, for it was he who said, 'Not Peter, but Christ, is the Rock.' And if you are resting in Him, trusting Him alone, however we may differ as to things ecclesiastical, we shall meet together in the air when the Lord Jesus comes!"

He stood there a moment, and then impulsively he threw both his arms around me and gave me a good squeeze—the only time in my life I have ever been hugged by a Roman Catholic priest!

We bade one another farewell. He went on to the monastery and I to my appointment. I have never seen him since, though I sent him the next day a copy of Mackay's book, *Grace and Truth*—a work that has brought blessing and light to thousands of souls.

But I dare to believe that I shall see my fellow traveler of that warm harvest day in the glory at the coming of our Lord Jesus and our gathering together unto Him.

11

SERVANT UNTO ALL

At eighteen minutes after five on the morning of April 18, 1906, San Francisco was shaken by a great earthquake. Fire, famine, and desolation followed. Across the bay tremors shook Oakland also, demolishing many buildings and damaging others.

The moment the earth heaved its crust the Ironside house in Oakland trembled. Helen, beside whom little Edmund was sleeping,* instinctively threw her body across him for his protection. Scarcely had she acted when the ceiling collapsed and the chimney, which ran up through the bedroom, crumbled, falling across her back. Harry was at her side instantly but not in time to save her from severe injury. As a result of this hapless experience Helen suffered violent headaches periodically for the rest of her life.

Because of the catastrophe Ironside interrupted his preaching ministry for two months so that he might do relief work in San Francisco and, at the same time, tell the gospel story to those whose spiritual needs were even greater than their physical necessities. When the most urgent demands of the calamity's aftermath were satisfied, he resumed his preaching schedule which took him away from home more and more.

*Eight-month old John was sleeping in a crib across the room.

It was at this time that Harry became acquainted with some of the early leaders among the Plymouth Brethren, among them A. E. Booth, Samuel Ridout, F. J. Enefer, and W. J. McClure. Before the earthquake Harry had met other Brethren giants, notably Paul J. Loizeaux, B. C. Greenman, and William M. Horsey, all of whom were participating in a Bible conference in San Francisco. Harry shared in the platform ministry for the first time.

Paul Loizeaux had great personal charm and was eloquent in the Scriptures. He was primarily an evangelist and Harry was drawn to him in a special way. One evening Harry went early to the meeting hall. He was standing at the rear of the auditorium in a little section separated from the rest of the hall by a partition, when two men arrived and entered the main auditorium. One of them asked the other, "Have you noticed the difference between the preaching of Loizeaux and Ironside?"

Harry knew he ought to make his presence known but, before he could think of what to say, the second man replied, "There's no way to compare the two; they are so utterly different."

It was too late now and, in an instant, the unwitting and embarrassed eavesdropper heard the first man say, "Yes, but there's one thing that stands out prominently. When Paul Loizeaux preaches, he's always telling people what they're going to get when they come to Christ. But Ironside is always telling them what they're going to get if they don't."

Harry was so struck with this contrast that he mentioned the conversation later on in the evening to Mr. Loizeaux, who said in his characteristic kindly way,

Paul J. Loizeaux, c. 1900

Arno C. Gaebelein, c. 1937

P. Daniel Loizeaux, c. 1950

Elie T. Loizeaux, 1976

"Well, my dear young brother, that is something to consider. We must never forget that our great business is to proclaim the grace of God."

Young Ironside loved his family dearly. An evening at home with Helen and the children was a cherished occasion. Yet even while he was enjoying his family he was convinced that he ought to be carrying the light of the gospel to those who were in darkness. Entries in his diary reflect this paradox, for example:

> In the evening at home together and had a nice time reading and listening to music, etc. Yet I feel rather condemned when loafing at home instead of being out preaching Christ.

In 1911 a fresh kind of testimony opened up, which occupied Ironside for about two months every autumn for more than a decade. This was a ministry to American Indians in their native villages in Arizona, southern California, and New Mexico—the Mojave, Laguna, Zuni, Hopi, Walapai, and Navajo tribes. He found them a receptive people and looked forward to his visits each year. Other Bible teachers who shared in this work sometimes were Arno C. Gaebelein and W. Leon Tucker. Gaebelein, the founder and for a half century editor of *Our Hope* magazine, and H. A. Ironside traveled more extensively as ambassadors for Christ during the first half of the twentieth century, and produced more Biblical literature than any others I can recall.

Harry was ill only a few times in his long and active career. When he was about seventy years of age he told me he could not remember ever having had a headache. However, after several weeks with the Laguna Indians in New Mexico one summer, he went to

Minneapolis where he was to preach two or three times. Somewhere along the way he picked up a toxic germ that forced him to remain in a Christian home in that city for six weeks with an attack of typhoid. He was very anxious to get home and at length, when he was scarcely strong enough to walk, he boarded a train for California. He felt obliged to engage a section in the Pullman car, where he stayed in his berth constantly except for meals. His progress to and from the dining car was unsteady, if not alarming.

During the day Harry would open the curtains of his berth. He reclined there, watching the scenery pass on the outside and the passengers go by on the inside, feeling somewhat like an oriental despot on a divan.

On the first morning, as he was reading his Bible, a rather buxom lady observed him and exclaimed, "Vat! You having vamily vorship all by yourselv? Vait!—I get mein Beibel and ve vorship togedder." In a few minutes she returned with her German Bible and the two began comparing the translations of the Epistle to the Hebrews, where the invalid had been reading. Not long afterward a tall, fair gentleman began walking past them. He stopped and then said, "Ah, reading the Bible? Vait a moment. I tank I get mine, too, and yoin with you"—and soon he returned with his Norwegian Bible. The lady was sitting on the edge of Ironside's berth, so the man took a seat across the aisle. As they were talking about the things of Christ, the Pullman conductor passed through the car and before many minutes others came to join the three. So many congregated that Harry had to raise his voice for all to hear him. After talking for more than an hour, he grew tired because of his weakened condition. So he excused himself, telling the people that he must rest for a while. Upon awaking from his nap he observed the Norwegian brother, who had been sitting near his berth.

"He's avake! He's avake!" that gentleman shouted out, and the message was passed along to other cars. Before long the whole audience had reassembled and Ironside began once more to expound Hebrews, emphasizing the gospel of Christ as much as he could and dwelling upon the Person of our Lord, the eternal Son. Some asked questions, from which it became evident that the great truths he had been discussing were new to a number of the passengers. Morning and afternoon each day were devoted to this "Bible conference," and it was an unwelcome hour to many when the train reached its destination.

Saying good-by and expressing her appreciation for the fellowship they had enjoyed, the German lady, remarking upon how her soul had been fed, asked, "Brudder, to vat denomination do you belong?"

With a twinkle in his eyes Harry said, "I belong to the same denomination that David did."

"Vat vas dat?" she inquired. "I did not know he belonged to any."

"David says," he replied, " 'I am a companion of all them that fear Thee and keep Thy precepts.' "

"Ya, Ya! Dat iss a vine denomination to belong to."

During his travels Ironside frequently did some writing—mostly of tracts and booklets. He usually worked on his expository writings at home. His first commentary was on the book of Esther,* which ap-

---

*Along with other Brethren writers of that era, Ironside's name did not appear on either the cover or the title page of his books but simply his initials—

peared in 1905, before he journeyed as often or as far as he was now doing. However, a book which was to have considerable impact for many years was composed in good part in Pullman cars and at Indian reservations—*Holiness, the False and the True*. It was published in 1912. The book tells of Harry's conversion at the age of fourteen, very much as it is recorded in an earlier chapter of this volume, and defines true holiness in contrast with that false holiness with which he had had experience in his Salvation Army days. There was a reluctance on Ironside's part to write the book because of his deep affection for the Army and some of its workers. But the conviction that the doctrine of holiness as they held it was unscriptural outweighed the hesitancy which natural courtesy suggested. *Holiness, the False and the True* has clarified the thinking of a multitude of God's people on the subject of personal sanctification.

Ironside's publisher was Loizeaux Brothers, in New York City. This firm, which was established in 1876, the year of Harry Ironside's birth, later published all but about fifteen of the more than ninety books, pamphlets, and tracts that HAI wrote. The publisher is widely known in evangelical circles today; in fact this biography is their production. The name appears early in Ironside's ministry, for one of the partners of Loizeaux Brothers was Paul J. Loizeaux, whom Harry met sometime around 1904. Loizeaux Brothers* and H.

HAI. In later years most of the Brethren began to identify themselves by name, and so did H. A. Ironside; for the reading public wants to know precisely whose books they are reading. However, Ironside became quite well known as HAI, and these initials will be used in this volume from time to time in reference to him.

*Timothy O. Loizeaux was associated with Paul in this venture; hence the firm name.

A. Ironside were fellow workers for Christ for nearly a half century.

From the time that young Ironside took up residence in one of Charles Montgomery's San Francisco hotels after resigning from the Salvation Army, he sensed a need among all God's people for Christian literature. He was convinced also of the importance of making gospel tracts available both to those who needed the gospel desperately as well as to some believers who would be willing to distribute them. It came to pass therefore that in 1912 he installed a book table in the Gospel Hall in Oakland. It was an immediate success. His own books, e.g., *Notes on the Book of Esther* and *Lectures on Daniel the Prophet*, were in demand, of course, and in addition to them the writings of other men, particularly by some of the Plymouth Brethren expositors. Consequently in 1914, after consulting with some of the brethren in Oakland, Harry decided to organize a bookstore to be called the Western Book and Tract Company.

> June 1, 1914
> A hard day—but a happy one in His service. Up at 6 and got breakfast for eight people—cleaned the dishes and went to town. Rented the store at 1817 Telegraph Avenue.

There would be no problem about establishing legitimate business credit. His publisher, the same distributor who had been supplying goods for the book table at the Gospel Hall, would serve him at the new store.

The Western Book and Tract Company opened on June 10, 1914. For more than a year the store's operation was beset with financial hardships of the severest kind. In the Lord's work as well as in secular business,

Mr. and Mrs. Ironside
with Edmund and John
Cape May, New Jersey,
1906. Dr. Ironside
called this photograph
"an archaeological gem"

The Gospel Auditorium, Oakland California, c. 1910

ventures that begin with little capital rarely prosper rapidly, if at all, a lesson Harry had to learn the hard way. He could not understand this. Had he not entered this ministry for Christ's sake? He himself expected to receive no profit from the enterprise. A few of his friends who had invested money in the company also had done this as a service for the Lord, and they were trusting Him to make the venture successful. Why were the financial burdens so heavy? His perplexity and impatience are reflected in his diary.

June 26, 1914

A very good day in the business, but yet a trying one for me as I am so constantly short of money. I have to plan all kinds of ways to get on. It seems strange—yet I know it is the Lord's dealing and I try to be content.

The first mention of the "depot" (a word frequently employed by HAI in referring to the store) in his diary follows:

July 23, 1914

A very perplexing day—much troubled in mind because of difficulties in connection with Tract Depot. Am trying hard to get all bills paid on time. . . .

Have met several very needy people today and do wish I had means to assist them.

August 6, 1914

One gets fair worn, waiting and hoping for what seems long deferred—the means to "provide things honest in the sight of all men." Today has tried me much but "I will trust, and not be afraid." . . . Thou knowest, O Lord.

October 14, 1914

My 38th birthday—surely more than half of life is done. Even though the Saviour's coming should not take place in my time, it would seem to be very near. Oh, to use the time that remains more for God than the time that is past!—The saints gave me a surprise supper at the Hall in the evening, and some acceptable gifts—one an envelope containing $52.00.

October 15, 1914

Many perplexing circumstances in connection with financial matters have made me feel the need of going slow, but
the help of last night meant a great deal. Got a $15.00 suit
today and a very good one for the money.

November 10, 1914

. . . Business cares weigh my spirit and I find it difficult to
rise above them. Lord, help me to confide in Thee more implicitly.

Ironside was primarily an itinerant Bible teacher,
not a sedentary bookstore proprietor. He was obliged
to travel a great deal, leaving the running of the depot
to volunteer helpers. Then God sent him a wonderful
gift—Miss Louise Deimel, who came to the store as an
employee several months after the Western Book and
Tract Company opened its doors, and stayed there for
many years, as long as the business continued. Harry
described her as "the right girl in the right place,"
which she surely was, bearing the burden of the work
in times of depression as well as of prosperity.

In the autumn of that same year HAI was returning
to California after several weeks' ministry in the east.
He was scheduled to visit the Laguna Indians along the
way and, on the train, became interested in observing
six Dominican sisters in animated conversation.* He
looked for an opportunity to talk with them and was
disappointed to hear them speaking in German, with
which he was not acquainted. He had about given up
hope when a young man at the far end of the coach took
a violin out of its case and started to play. Other
passengers put aside whatever they were doing and

---

*In telling elsewhere of this experience (*Random Reminiscences*, Loizeaux
Brothers, Inc., 1939) Ironside states that there were eight nuns. This is
doubtless due to lapse of memory. The number six has been taken directly
from his diary, as written on the date of the adventure.

began to hum or to sing as the violinist played tunes familiar to them. In time he hit upon a German melody which was known to the nuns, and some of them sang the words to his accompaniment. The song was familiar to Harry also, for several German Mennonite missionaries, who worked among the Indians, had translated some of their hymns into the Hopi tongue. It was such a hymn that was being rendered now by this strange choir, and Harry, enjoying it, must have evinced his pleasure unconsciously, for the older nun (the other five were quite young) leaned toward him and spoke in excellent English.

"These dear children! They enjoy this so much. You see, we are German nuns on our way to California. Our convent at home was destroyed during the war, and we are going out into a new country. I think of these young sisters as my children, for I am the Mother Superior. They are so homesick! Everything is so different here, and that melody has stirred them deeply, for it reminds them of the old country. They were a part of the convent choir at home." She seemed to expect Ironside to reply, for she kept looking at him interrogatively.

Delighted at this opportunity he responded, telling her that he too was familiar with the song they were singing. He explained that he knew neither the German nor English words, but that he had heard the Hopi Indians sing the hymn in their own language.

"Do you mean," she inquired, "that there are some of those dark people, the American Indians, with whom you are acquainted, who really know and love our Lord Jesus Christ?"

Thrilled with the question—for she certainly spoke as one who knew Christ herself—HAI told her that

A Group of Brethren Evangelists and Teachers
Left to Right: Wm. Haig, A. E. Booth, C. Crain, F. J. Enefer,
H. A. Ironside, B. C. Greenman
Kneeling and Sitting: R. E. McAllister, Nels Thompson,
E. K. Bailey

H. A. Ironside
Ministering in the
Canadian Northwest
c. 1904

there were many genuine Christians among the Indian tribes. As soon as the violinist ceased playing, therefore, Sister Gregoria asked Harry if he would be willing to tell the nuns something about the work, if she would act as his interpreter. To this he assented eagerly.

Of course, in describing the missionary work among the Indians, Ironside was solicitous to bring into his tale the gospel of salvation in Christ and justification by faith. He was careful to avoid contention or criticism. When he had concluded his "lecture," Sister Gregoria asked him if he were a missionary himself. He replied that he was one who gave his full time to preaching the gospel and that this was how he happened to know something of the work among the Indians, as for a number of years he had devoted several months a year to visiting and preaching Christ to them.

"I do hope," the Mother Superior said, "that you are a good Catholic."

"Though I cannot claim any goodness of my own," he replied, "I can assure you that I am a member of the holy catholic Church, purchased by our Lord Jesus Christ with His own blood."

This brought questions, of course, and Harry, remembering that the Apostle Paul said, "I am all things to all men," alluded to the writings of some of the Roman Catholic fathers, as he explained how unrighteous sinners obtain righteousness through faith and that they are made fit for God's holy presence by grace alone. He showed them, for example, how St. Bernard of Clairvaux had exclaimed when he was dying, "Holy, holy Jesus, Thy wounds are my merits!"

"You astonish me," Sister Gregoria said. "You seem

to be familiar with all the saints, most unusual for one who is not a Roman Catholic."

"Oh, but you see," he replied, "I try to familiarize myself with all of them, for all the saints belong to me, and I belong to them. More than that, through the infinite grace of the Lord Jesus Christ I myself am a saint!"

"A saint!" she cried out in amazement. *"Kinder!"* she exclaimed in German to the younger nuns, and spoke quickly and excitedly, words that Ironside was sure were something like this, "Children! It seems hardly possible for me to believe my ears, but this man says that he himself is a saint!"

It was their turn to look at him in astonishment— which they did. Surely they thought that all the saints were dead, but here was a man who was very much alive and claimed to be one. They showed clearly by their amused glances at him that they considered him to be just a little out of his mind. But this gave him the very opportunity he wanted—to show from the Bible that a saint is one who has been set apart by and is separated to God through the precious blood of Christ, through His atoning work on the cross, and that all who have put their trust in Him as the Son of God and Saviour from sin are called saints in His Word. He referred to passage after passage, which Sister Gregoria, in turn, interpreted for her "children."

So all through the day they plied him with questions which he answered gladly. As they separated at Albuquerque, it was with the acknowledgment that all of them had been edified by the things of Christ which were discussed. Harry felt assured that their hearts had been receptive to the truth of God's Word, which will not return unto Him void.

12

ABOUT THE FATHER'S BUSINESS

By the year 1915 Lillian Watson, Harry's half-sister, had grown to young womanhood. Ironside was genuinely fond of her and frequently, when he was called upon to cross by ferry to San Francisco, where Lillian lived, he would try to see her. Sometimes they would have luncheon together. Then too, Lillian occasionally visited the Ironsides in Oakland for an afternoon, or an overnight stay when Harry and Helen were away and wanted someone to stay with the two boys.

In the spring Harry began to suspect that Lillian was becoming romantically attached. He writes in his diary of a Mr. Laidlaw who came over to Oakland with her one evening. Again, "Lillian and Mr. Laidlaw had tea with Helen today."

Robert A Laidlaw was known widely in New Zealand as a rising young businessman of Auckland. He was equally well known in the United States and Britain as an able expositor of the Scriptures. In fellowship with the Plymouth Brethren, Bert Laidlaw was the author of a gospel tract, *The Reason Why*, which in time reached a distribution total of more than ten million copies in the English-speaking world.

Harry was at home during the latter part of April. A page in his diary reads:

April 28, 1915

Well, it looks as though I am to lose my only sister. Bert Laidlaw came over today to "ask" me for Lillian, and if they wed he will take her to New Zealand in three months! The Lord guide.

It is not clear when the Lord revealed His mind to Harry. No further mention is made in his journal until three months later. Perhaps HAI was slow to understand God's will or else reluctant to reach a decision in so important a matter, especially in view of the fact that, if the marriage should take place, Lillian would be living on the other side of the world. In July things moved rapidly.

July 19, 1915

Robert and Lillian were with us all night and left at noon for San Francisco. I suppose I will only see them once again, and that to marry them next Monday night—then never perhaps until "the day breaks and the shadows flee away" at "the coming of the Lord Jesus and our gathering together unto Him."

One feels a bit queer about it—but I hope Lillian will be very happy.

July 26, 1915

I married Lillian and Robert Laidlaw, with James Arthur as best man, and Carol Gibsen and Clarabel West as bridesmaids. A happy reception downstairs afterwards.

Only a few days later the Laidlaws sailed for New Zealand. Their visits to the United States were rare.

During the next fourteen years, from 1916 to 1929, Ironside accomplished more than five men of lesser energy and zeal could have done in their entire lives. As nearly as I can estimate he preached the gospel and expounded the Scriptures about 6,500 times to an aggregate audience of 1,125,000 people. It was necessary for him to travel thousands of miles to do this, to take no vacations, and to keep going in weariness and sometimes sickness, for this was before radio came into use as a means of spreading the Word of God.

All this time the Lord kept His servant from disaster even in perilous experiences. Several such occasions come to mind: one, when a train on which HAI was traveling was brought to a halt only a few hundred yards from a washed-out bridge; another, when he was spared in a hotel fire; and still another when he was struck down, but not injured, by a speeding motorcycle. He must have been exposed to still other hazards, some of which only God is aware.

During these years Ironside's writing ministry continued to grow. Four Bible expositions were written in this period, plus a score of shorter works. In addition, Harry was speaking two or three times a day and directing the Western Book and Tract Company by mail.

Whereas many of his engagements in the early years had been at denominational and independent churches, by far the major portion of HAI's speaking appointments were in Brethren assemblies. He had always felt evangelism to be God's highest calling, yet little by little his messages became almost exclusively expository, with a gospel note added whenever the Holy Spirit led him in this way.

The enlarged platform witness may in part be traced to an invitation that came to him from Dr. George McPherson, who directed the Old Tent Evangel in New York City. In 1918 Ironside began what became a two-week summer ministry in McPherson's tent. This was carried on annually for eight years. As a result of these meetings he came into contact with many well-known Christian workers who, in turn, invited or recommended him to other places of witness.

In the same year, too, Brethren assemblies united in engaging the St. James M. E. Church in Elizabeth, New Jersey, for ten days of meetings, at which HAI was the speaker. Inasmuch as this conference was supported by all the Brethren of that particular fellowship in the state and vicinity, large crowds gathered and there were evidences that quite a number of men and women were brought to the knowledge of Christ as their personal Saviour in this campaign. Many believers were built up in the Christian faith.

Like a mailman who goes for a long walk on his day off, whenever Harry had a free evening he could be found attending a service wherever he might be, whether at home or on the road. He had an intense love for the Word of God and was almost always stimulated when he heard other speakers expound it. His diaries contain many brief entries such as these: "Heard Billy Sunday tonight"; "Listened to William Jennings Bryan"; "Heard A. B. Simpson"; "A. C. Gaebelein spoke," etc. Other distinguished ministers are named in similar ways, e.g., James M. Gray, P. W. Philpott, Lewis Sperry Chafer, A. H. Stewart. Among several hundred such entries in the diary I found only four indications that Harry was not instructed or blessed by a message. Twice he wrote: "Was disappointed"; once, ". . . twaddle by a Baptist preacher from Chicago"; and the fourth time, "Mr. ————of the Y.M.C.A. spoke but it was poor stuff. We need to pray for him." Usually remarks of this kind were made: "A splendid message"; "Philpott was exceptionally good"; "It was a great address."

Whereas HAI had the capacity for deep friendship,

he was denied the joy of many of them because he was rarely in one place more than a few days, days filled with pursuance of the Father's business. However, in 1914 a rare intimacy began at a Bible conference at Mt. Hermon, California, where Harry shared a week's ministry with James A. Sutherland, pastor of Calvary Baptist Church of San Jose. The warm friendship between these two men of God continued through many years. In fact, Ironside told me that he traced his call to the Moody Memorial Church* of Chicago in 1930 to the interposition of Jim Sutherland.

By 1924 Sutherland had become a member of the Extension Staff of the Moody Bible Institute.** He persuaded Harry to accept meetings under the Institute's direction. As a consequence Ironside spent part of his winters in Florida, teaching the Scriptures as a Moody Bible Institute speaker, and summers at one Bible conference after another under the same aegis. During the spring and the autumn HAI engaged himself elsewhere, as a result of direct invitations from Brethren assemblies as well as from local churches throughout the United States and Canada. He was now speaking about 500 times annually.

For several years, beginning in 1924, Ironside lectured for two months to the students of Dallas Theological Seminary (then known as Evangelical Theological College) in Dallas, Texas. Lewis Sperry Chafer, president of the seminary, was anxious to have

*The Moody Church is the complete name of the corporation. The title, The Moody Memorial Church, is a name given to the building as a tribute to D. L. Moody.

**The Moody Bible Institute and The Moody Church are in close fellowship. They are not, however, organically affiliated.

him join the faculty as a full-time member. Harry was to be there seven months a year, with allowance for reasonable absences for outside engagements provided classroom work could be rescheduled for such times. He would still be free for five months a year for itinerant ministry on his own.

At first Dr. Chafer's offer appealed to Harry—he would be instructing dedicated young men; he and Helen could have a home in Dallas, which would permit them to enjoy married life as it was meant to be; there would be time for study and writing; and his ministry across the land would not be entirely curtailed. But after some months of prayer, he wrote to Chafer that he thought the proposed arrangement would be a mistake. Helen wanted to remain in Oakland to be with John until he should obtain his academic and doctoral degrees from the University of California (Berkeley), where he was at that time a junior. Harry wondered if, as he wrote, "I could be satisfied to be tied down after having so wide and varied an itinerant ministry for so many years." Furthermore, there was the matter of the Western Book and Tract Company. The bookstore was doing fairly well by this time, but Ironside rightly felt a responsibility to a number of friends who had invested somewhere around $35,000 in the business. He thought he could do much more on behalf of the company if he continued traveling as he had been doing. So he declined the offer and the matter was settled.

The Ironside family experienced some changes during these years. The boys were no longer children and there was now a daughter, Lillian. Edmund had been just old enough to enter the army in World War I, during which he was married to Miss Mabel Guthrie. In

1920 a daughter, Lillian, was born from this union. But young Mrs. Ironside was quite ill and shortly after the baby's birth Harry and Helen took the little girl into their home. In time, with the full consent of both Edmund and Mabel, she was legally adopted by her grandparents as their daughter. Mabel died of tuberculosis not long afterwards.

Edmund had wandered away from the Lord and was engaged in business in Florida. There he married again in 1926, his second wife being Miss Freda Banford of Montreal. In the great hurricane of 1928 they lost everything they had in the world but, through the experience, gained everything that is of worth—both for time and for eternity. Edmund was wonderfully restored to the Lord and before long set out for Dallas, where he took some special courses at Dallas Theological Seminary. God gave the Edmund Ironsides two lovely daughters—Marion and Enid, both born there in Dallas.*

Edmund's heart was with the black people, and within a year he founded and became the superintendent of Southern Bible Institute, a Bible school with a student body composed of blacks, where he remained until his death in 1941.

Meanwhile John, who had been a bright Christian, went into a spiritual eclipse in his senior year at the University of California. He graduated with an A.B. degree in 1927 and did not pursue his studies toward a

---

*Edmund's widow, Freda Ironside, currently (1976) lives in Woodstock, New Brunswick, Canada, with her younger daughter, Enid, and Enid's husband, Pastor James Webber. Marion, Freda's older daughter, is the wife of Allen Crawford, pastor of Faith Community Church, Roslyn, Pennsylvania. The last couple HAI ever married was Allen Crawford and Marion Ironside in Wheaton, Illinois, on September 2, 1950.

doctorate. Rather, in great perplexity he delved into a variety of spurious cults and philosophies. His doubts as to the reality of spiritual things caused his father and mother much heaviness of heart.

In December 1929 Ironside held a series of services in the Moody Church. Then, after nearly eleven months' absence from home, he arrived in Oakland on December twenty-second. There he found another invitation from Dr. Chafer—not this time to become a permanent full-time faculty member but to become a member of the Board of Regents, and on December twenty-seventh he wired his acceptance. This was the first of many directorships he held.*

The seven-year period ended on a happy note, for the diary of December 31, 1929 reads:

> Had watchnight service 8—12 midnight in the Gospel Auditorium here in Oakland, brethren George W. Hunter, T. Carroll, and Elliott McAllister participating.

*For a complete list of organizations with which H. A. Ironside was affiliated, see Appendix B.

13

FOR HIS NAME'S SAKE

The year 1930 was an epochal one in the life of Harry Ironside, not only because he delivered 653 messages from the Word of God and had the joy of seeing hundreds profess to believe in the Lord Jesus Christ as their Saviour, but also because by God's grace it marked another milestone in his service of love in Christ's name.

The year began in the same place it ended—in the Oakland Gospel Auditorium as the Watch Night Service came to its close, and in his home in reunion with his beloved family for a few days. Then, his diary reveals, in an almost incredibly short time he felt the need to leave his family again.

> January 4, 1930
>
> Left Oakland for Los Angeles this morning—arriving at 11:40 P.M. Staying at the Bible Institute. Am here to conduct a two-weeks' Bible Conference in the Glendale Presbyterian Church, and also to give some addresses at the Institute.
>
> Hard to leave the family with whom I have had only two weeks after an absence of practically eleven months—but it is "for His Name's sake" that "I am a stranger in the earth."

Harry was able to get back to Oakland for two days before it was necessary for him to leave again for an extended trip which would include series of meetings in Chicago, Racine, Augusta, St. Louis, and Galveston by the end of March. Before retiring on the night prior to his departure he wrote again of the hardship that separation from his loved ones imposed upon him.

> January 28, 1930
>
> Had good visit with my folks after the meeting tonight. It is going to be hard to leave tomorrow, but it is "for His Name's sake."

Ironside was never free of this longing to be with his family, nor of his loneliness without them. He never lost consciousness that in the normal course of life a man's place and duty are with his family. This is illustrated by a letter I received from him several years later when I wrote to inquire about Mrs. Ironside's health after she had suffered a severe coronary occlusion.

> December 16, 1939
>
> My dear Brother:
>
> Thanks for your letter. It is always good to hear from you. Mrs. Ironside has been making steady progress, and now the doctor feels she should go to a hospital for X ray and some tests; so I am going to take her over to Geneva today. We shall know a little later just how things are.
>
> I do wish I did not have to be away so much while she is ill, but that is one of the trials of the path which one must endure while seeking to minister Christ to others. I often feel like saying with the bride in the Song of Solomon, "They made me the keeper of the vineyards, but my own vineyard have I not kept."

After a stopover at Albuquerque, Ironside proceeded eastward. February second fell on a Sunday in 1930. HAI was on the train en route to Chicago, and this troubled him:

> February 2, 1930
>
> Sorry that circumstances seemed to make it necessary to be on the train for the Lord's day. I dislike this very much and had hoped I might have stayed in Albuquerque at least for the Lord's Supper—but was afraid No. 2 might be late

getting into Chicago. However, I feel worn and half-sick, so perhaps it is just as well that I can lie here and doze. Hope to be rested up when I get to my destination tomorrow night, D.V.

The train was late but caused no inconvenience, and Ironside began his ministry at the Founder's Week Conference, promoted by and held at the Moody Bible Institute every year. During the week he had an interview with James M. Gray, president of the Institute, in which Dr. Gray urged upon him a more permanent connection with M.B.I. But Harry was not certain that this was the Lord's will and suggested that they carry on for the present with the arrangement already in operation—HAI to assist at Moody conferences when invited and if he was free to accept.

Following the Founder's Week Conference Ironside was engaged for a series of meetings at Wheaton College, Wheaton, Illinois. An important interview took place at this time. It is noted briefly in the diary:

> February 17, 1930
>
> An exceedingly full day. After breakfast and devotions wrote a number of letters. Then down town [in Chicago] for a conference with Thomas S. Smith and another elder of the Moody Church, relative to possibly being called to be the minister there.

HAI had visited the Moody Church on three occasions prior to this, for a series of Bible studies. The first time was one month after the new $1,000,000 building was completed in 1925. P. W. Philpott was the pastor of the church at that time and invited Ironside for two weeks. But Dr. Philpott was called away to Winnipeg during the engagement and asked Harry to remain for a third week, which he did. He visited the church again the following year, in December 1929, an appointment already mentioned.

Some seven months prior to this interview with Smith, a committee from the Moody Church had waited upon Ironside and asked him if he would consider accepting a call to be its pastor, since Dr. Philpott had resigned. Harry answered then with a decisive, "No!" He could not entertain such a suggestion for a moment! He felt utterly unqualified for the position; but more important than that, his views as to the Christian ministry, views held generally by Plymouth Brethren, did not fit in with becoming the pastor of a church. However, HAI now began to sense that perhaps it might be the will of God for him to consider the call seriously. He prayed a great deal about it. If he should accept the call, would he be repudiating what he had long believed and taught about the ministry? More and more it seemed to impress itself upon him that the opportunity was a definite call from God. Yet he hesitated—his convictions long held against a one-man ministry, his fear that he might not satisfy the congregation, and his inexperience in administrative work seeming to erect a barrier against accepting the call. On the other hand, he thought, it was not a one-man ministry, after all, for Moody Church had two assistant pastors who helped in various ways—calling on the membership, attending the business details, overseers of various responsibilities. The people there had been blessed through his teaching of the Word on his visits and they seemed to want him. The Moody Church was directed by an official board of fifty-five men, who would be able to advise in administrative matters.

Finally Harry concluded that he might be able to accept without compromising his conscientious convictions regarding ordination by man and other things. Therefore he told Thomas Smith that he would put the question to a test. The matter was to be placed before the executive committee of the church. If the executive committee was absolutely unanimous in wishing him to accept the call, he would permit them to put his name before the congregation, and the same stipulation should apply to the congregational meeting—if the vote should be absolutely unanimous, he would accept the call for one year's trial.

A week later HAI was in Racine, Wisconsin. He had returned to his hotel room after an evening service when he received a telephone call. His diary entry tells the story:

> February 24, 1930
>
> At 10:30 the phone rang. Long distance—Chicago calling. Mr. Herring [assistant pastor of Moody Church] notified me that I was unanimously called to be pastor of the Moody Church. I go in tomorrow to talk it over.

This overture was that of the executive committee. The congregational meeting was yet to be held.

> February 25, 1930
>
> A hectic day, yet very satisfactory. Left for Chicago at 7:45 A.M. In conference for nearly two and a half hours with leaders in the Moody Church. A very blessed spirit prevailed and I am happy over the prospects of intimate association with them.
>
> Saw Jim Sutherland in the afternoon.

Sutherland and Ironside had discussed at some length the possibility of the call and had prayed about it.

From Chicago Harry went to Augusta, Georgia, his first visit to that city and his diary of March 5 states:

> Tonight the Moody Church votes on my nomination as pastor. Later—Wire received at 11:20 P.M. from Ass't. Pastor Porter telling me the church called me unanimously.

H. A. Ironside with Thomas S. Smith
Long-Time Elder of Moody Church, 1935

Harry sent a telegram in reply, accepting the call. The conditions stipulated by him were to hold: it was to be a one-year trial. Further, it had been agreed that should the decision be in the affirmative on both sides, he must fulfill appointments to which he had committed himself throughout the month of August. He would have only a few Sundays free in the meantime—March 16 and then, beginning on April 27, a period of eight weeks with the exception of two Sundays. All these he would give to the Moody Church, becoming its pastor on March 16 but not assuming full duties until September 6.

It was only ten days, then, from his call to his next visit to Chicago. Of that initial appearance as pastor in the pulpit where there had been such illustrious servants of the Lord as Dwight L. Moody, Reuben A. Torrey, A. C. Dixon, Paul Rader, and P. W. Philpott as his predecessors, let his diary speak again:

March 16, 1930

My first Lord's day as pastor of the Moody Church.

At 9:15 A.M. a few of us broke bread in the feast of remembrance in church study.

At 10:45 I preached on 1 Corinthians 2:2. 3,500 were present and there was a serious impression.

Dinner with the Herrings.

At 5:50 I spoke briefly to the C. C. Club in Torrey Hall, on "Life at Best."

At 7:30 I preached on "God's Salvation and the Scorner's Doom"—2 Kings 7, to about 3,700 people. Five confessed Christ.

It seemed a further token of God's gracious pleasure.

PART 4

THE MOODY CHURCH YEARS

"If any man speak, let him speak as the oracles of God;
if any man minister, let him do it as of
the ability which God giveth: that God
in all things may be glorified through Jesus Christ,
to whom be praise and dominion for ever and ever.
Amen."

1 PETER 4:11

"Beside those things that are without,
that which cometh upon me daily,
the care of all the churches."

2 CORINTHIANS 11:28

14

THE HUSBANDMAN MUST LABOR

There was an interval of six weeks between Harry Ironside's first Sunday as pastor of the Moody Church and his second Lord's day there. The time was spent in Texas—first in Galveston, where for a long time he had been booked for two weeks of Bible-teaching ministry, and then on to Dallas where, in addition to a month's teaching at Dallas Theological Seminary, he had preaching appointments every Sunday and five nights a week. Despite the fact that his schedule always accelerated in Dallas, Harry welcomed his visits there. It was exciting to have the opportunity of teaching appreciative students, young men who would themselves be entering the ministry in a short time; he had great affection for Dr. Chafer and his associates at the seminary; and to go to Dallas meant that he would have a reunion with Edmund and his lovely family.

Ironside always had a love for music, especially the old gospel songs. It was a special treat for him when a talented vocal soloist sang a musical message immediately preceding his own message from the Word of God. Harry's journals are punctuated with commendatory remarks concerning those who shared his services in this way from time to time. Among his favorites was a soprano whom he had first heard at Wheaton College in Illinois—Thelma Johnson. He used to speak of her as a Swedish nightingale. Another pet of his was Stratton Shufelt, minister of music at Moody Church as well as the soloist for nine years.

When Ironside went to Texas in 1930 he obtained engagements for Thelma Johnson (by that time Mrs. Porrit) to be his soloist at all his public services during the six weeks he was to be there.

It was characteristic of HAI to be scrupulous, not only in avoiding evil itself but even the slightest appearance of it. He therefore arranged that Thelma should travel to and fro between Chicago and Dallas on different trains from those he would take, and that she should be entertained in homes of ministers or friends in the vicinity where he would be preaching. He wanted no one to find any occasion for gossip.

The Texas ministry concluded in Dallas on April 25 after a staggering schedule of 67 messages in twenty-five days. Ironside arrived in Chicago on Saturday night, the twenty-sixth, and Sunday he began his second Lord's day services at Moody Church. That night he wrote in his diary:

> April 27, 1930
>
> It seems good indeed to be back at Moody Memorial. I am happy to be trusted by God for this great work.
>
> At 9:30 A.M. five of us broke bread in remembrance of the Lord—in my study.
>
> At 10:10 A.M. I lectured to the Friendly Bible Class on 1 Thessalonians 1.
>
> At 11 A.M. preached on "The Things That Are Made and His Workmanship—God's Two Great Epic Poems."
>
> Out to Brother Tom Smith's for dinner, then at 3 back to the hotel for an afternoon nap. Raining when I awoke.
>
> Raining at night—only about 2,000 present. Preached on

"The Brazen Serpent and the Uplifted Saviour." Several in Inquiry Room.

The first time I visited the Moody Church was in the mid-thirties. HAI took me way upstairs to his study, a delightful hideout lined with books. I was fascinated by this secluded place and used to tease him, saying that the real reason he accepted the call to the church was on account of the study. Years later I was amused to discover in his diary that I was not so far wrong in my conjecture as might be supposed! Here is the entry of the Monday following his second Sunday as Moody's pastor:

> April 28, 1930
>
> Have had a most interesting and really restful day. Spent hours fitting up my study in the Moody Church—one of the coziest nooks for a student I have ever seen.
>
> Then wrote about 30 letters, partly dictated and partly by hand.
>
> At night had cafeteria supper in the church and attended my first meeting of the committee who manages everything.
>
> It seemed strange not to be preaching. I need some days like this occasionally, when change of work proves real rest.

Of course Harry's acceptance of the call to the pastorate was based on much more than a cozy nook! Yet that room was a great joy to him. It was the first oasis he ever had that he could claim entirely for himself as a library and place for private meditation and study. It was there, too, that every Sunday morning at 8 o'clock for some years he commemorated the Lord's death with several brethren of like mind.

The Moody Church has always been mission oriented. At the time Harry Ironside became its pastor there were ninety-two of its own members on mission fields in twenty-eight different countries. Sixty-seven of them received their complete financial support from the church and most of the others a fair portion of their maintenance from church contributions. One of the most important weeks of the Moody Church year is its annual missionary conference.

In 1930 the scheduled missionary rally began only a few days after the new pastor's arrival from Texas. Like the conferences in earlier years, it was used by God as a means of calling some young men and women to serve Him wherever He might direct them, and of stirring others to prayer and the giving of their means so that the gospel of Christ might reach to the uttermost part of the earth. Harry was thrilled with the response. His diary entry at the close of the final day reflects this.

> May 6, 1930
>
> A great victory here on the Lord's day. $50,000 over-subscribed, and only fifteen minutes of morning and fifteen minutes of night meeting devoted to money raising. "The people had a mind to give."
>
> Nor was the spiritual side disturbed. Scores offered themselves for service and six professed to be saved at night.

Succeeding weeks set a general pattern that HAI followed during the eighteen years he was associated with Moody Church. He would usually leave Chicago late Sunday night or early Monday morning to preach somewhere in the United States or Canada, returning to Chicago the next Saturday morning. As a rule Saturdays and any other weekdays that he was in Chicago were taken up with correspondence, committee meetings, and callers at the church.

Because of commitments Harry had made months before he accepted the Moody call, he left Chicago toward the end of June 1930 for a round of summer Bible conferences: Gull Lake, Cedar Lake, Eaglesmere, Montrose, Ocean Grove, and Colorado Springs. Finally, after seven weeks' absence, he returned to Oakland. The night of his arrival he spoke in the Gospel Auditorium.

Eight wonderful days were spent at home before he had to go to Chicago to take up full duties of the pastorate. Then he bade farewell to the believers in Oakland. Because circumstances were such that Helen Ironside and Lillian could not yet accompany him, HAI departed alone once again. He took residence in the Plaza Hotel, located across the street from the church, where his small family would join him later. However, just the day before Harry left Oakland, John, who had taken a position with the Dollar Steamship Company back in June, returned home after his first round-the-world trip. Father and son had a happy reunion for almost twenty-four hours.

Besides Harry's new church relationship there were still other events to make the year memorable for him. In June Wheaton College conferred an honorary degree on him, Doctor of Letters. The former Salvation Army lad was now Henry Allan Ironside, Litt. D.

Some of the Plymouth Brethren had been displeased when HAI accepted the call of Moody Church. They felt that in so doing Harry had turned his back on a conviction he had held for many years. They were opposed to what some of them termed a one-man ministry, and it was also contrary to their view that a servant of the Lord should receive a stipulated salary for preaching the Word of God.

Of course Ironside had weighed thoughtfully objections of this nature before accepting Moody Church's invitation. He had put out the fleece and seemed to have an affirmative answer from the Lord. He could

not ignore the importance and opportunity of the proposed ministry and concluded that it was from God.
He had peace about his decision and, as the months rolled by, there were many evidences of God's pleasure.

As to a one-man ministry, HAI had changed the title
of the two assistant pastors—Harry Herring and
Charles A. Porter—to Associate Pastor; for whereas,
to be sure, theirs was not the major preaching ministry
of the church, what they were doing in the way of
visitation, counseling, the business of the church, and
other Christian services was equally as much God-
given activity as was his own work there.

When the matter of receiving a stated salary for
preaching was mentioned, Harry used to say, with a
twinkle in his eyes, "I accept a salary for ad-
ministrating a $100,000 corporation. I throw in the
preaching for nothing!"

Despite the ripple of criticism about his pastorship
and honorary degree, Ironside never lost his esteem
for the Plymouth Brethren. He admired them for their
doctrinal stability and held them in affection as his
brothers and sisters in Christ. As long as he lived
Harry thought of himself as one of them. On such rare
occasions as he happened to be free on a Sunday morning, he sought out a Brethren assembly where he
might worship the Lord and break bread in remembrance of Him in fellowship with some of these dear
saints.

Another important event marked 1930. In August,
while Harry was attending the General Bible Conference at Montrose, Pennsylvania, as one of the
speakers, he was appointed director of the Montrose
Bible Conference Association to succeed its founder,

Dr. Reuben A. Torrey, upon whose invitation he had first gone to Montrose.

But now it was Sunday, September 6, 1930. Dr. Ironside was back in Chicago to assume the responsibilities of shepherding Christ's fold in the Moody Church, with its membership of about 3,500, an auditorium seating 4,040 persons, and its many activities at home and abroad.

September 6, 1930

The Lord's day dawned cool and cloudy.

In the A.M. over 3,000 present—a communion service. I preached on "Proclaiming the Lord's Death Till He Come."

In the afternoon went to Brother Burk's Grace and Truth Chapel, packed with about 300, and spoke on "The Father's House and the Kingdom."

At night we had about 3,500 and God was with us in power. A number confessed Christ at the close—some were apparently exceedingly bright and gave us great joy.

The evident blessing upon his work seemed another token of divine approval of the present and an earnest of things to come. The record of Harry's first fifty-two Sundays at the church reveals that there was not one on which someone was not led to Christ. Harry was not a great one for counting numbers. Furthermore he was particular, even with himself, not to claim conversions without some clear evidence that it was true regeneration. Generally his diary entries read that such-and-such a number *professed* to be saved, or *indicated* that they had received Christ, or *appeared* to have made a decision for the Lord. The diaries show no groups of fifties or hundreds coming forward to confess the Lord Jesus Christ as Saviour, but there is consistency in response to the gospel week after week. Here are some examples of Ironside's comments in his journals:

Fifteen confessed Christ tonight.

> Six or more professed to come to Christ. A fine audience and several in Inquiry Room. Only one lady made a profession tonight.

I think it is safe to say that during the eighteen years HAI preached the Word in Moody Church, very few Sundays passed without some unredeemed sinners turning to the Saviour.

The Moody pulpit afforded Ironside an even wider audience than its large membership supplied. Hundreds of students of the Moody Bible Institute worshiped there on the Lord's day and, for a period of four years, the Institute's radio station WMBI broadcast the church's Sunday morning service. Later the church purchased radio time, first from Chicago's WAIT, and after that from Station WJJD. The support for these broadcasts over commercial stations came voluntarily from listeners in large portions of Illinois, Wisconsin, and Indiana, and also from some places in Ohio and Iowa.

The worldwide interests and activities of the Moody Church make it a meeting place, a forwarding address, and a haven for many servants of the Lord. This was the case no less during the leadership of H. A. Ironside than it is today. In his first four months as pastor his study door opened to distinguished visitors from across the United States and abroad. I counted in HAI's diary for September through December 1930 the names of seventy-eight visitors of recognized high spiritual stature. It was a new experience, too, for Harry Ironside to be in a position to pass out favors. The one suggestion that came to him most often astonished him greatly, as an excerpt from his diary reveals.

It amazes me how many of the brethren write requesting an opportunity to preach at Moody Memorial.

On December seventh a committee from the church waited upon HAI and asked if he would rescind his condition to remain as pastor for one year's trial only. Would he not stay indefinitely? He said he would weigh the matter and pray about it, but he did not give an immediate answer. Yet three days later he was so convinced that he was in the place of the Lord's appointment that he told the committee he would consent to stay on as long as they wanted him, or until the Lord should indicate to him that it was time for a change.

The final day of 1930 brought happy reunion with Mrs. Ironside and Lillian, who arrived from Oakland to take up residence with HAI at the Plaza Hotel. With great joy the three went to the Watch Night Meeting, where Helen was introduced to the congregation. Two messages were delivered during the service. Ernest M. Wadsworth spoke first, on "Revival." Then, as midnight approached, Dr. Ironside followed with a message entitled, "The Unknown Future." Upon getting back to the hotel he wrote on the final page of his 1930 diary:

December 31, 1930

Just as the new year dawned four came to Christ in the Inquiry Room.

15

HOLDING FORTH THE WORD OF LIFE

It is no small accomplishment to draw an audience of about 4,000 people Sunday morning after Sunday morning and almost as many on Sunday evenings. Harry Ironside did this in the Moody Church for the greater part of eighteen years. He did it apart from the use of dramatic sermon titles or so-called added attractions but simply by expounding the Scriptures.

Ironside was not really a topical preacher. He was a verse-by-verse Bible expositor. Because in certain quarters custom fancied that the subject matter of sermons appear in newspaper notices and church bulletins, he would give out sermon titles in advance. They were nothing more than convenient allusions to passages of Scripture. Suppose his announced topic was "Poor Gallio." The message would be an exposition of Acts 18, beginning at verse 12. "Assurance by the Word" might be HAI's designation of the whole fifth chapter of First John. I recall a message that was advertised as "God Revealed in Christ." It was a comparison between and meditation upon John 1:18 and Hebrews 1:3. If he had been asked to announce a title of an address he was planning to make on Exodus 35 (which has to do with gifts for the Tabernacle), he might have said, "Oh, call it 'Cords and Pins.' " His address would follow his usual style—a verse-by-verse exposition of the chapter.

It has been said that HAI was the despair of many professors of homiletics; for not infrequently, when an instructor would emphasize some rule of the science of preaching, a student might say, "Dr. Ironside doesn't do it that way." No, he didn't do it that way. Dr. Ironside had a way all his own.

Ironside was saturated with the Scriptures. No tedious hours needed to be spent preparing a message. I cannot recollect a single entry in his diaries that mentions sermon preparation. However, behind every message there were years of study. For one hour every day he had his own early "morning watch." This hour was devoted to intense study of the Bible and prayer.

Perhaps there are some who have tired of hearing HAI, but I never met such a person. His associate pastors and elders must have listened to him hundreds and hundreds of times at Moody Church. Others traveled from Bible conference to Bible conference where he spoke. Still others sat at his feet in theological seminaries and Bible institutes; and others, like the author, listened to him expound the Word of God and read his writings for decades without ever wearying of them but rather being refreshed by them. A conservative count of the messages he delivered during the span of his Moody Church years would be around 7,500. Anyone who knew HAI would agree with me, I think, that he doubtless approached the pulpit the 7,500th time with as much eagerness and enthusiasm as he did the first time.

Dr. Ironside was an evangelical Christian. He

Moody Memorial Church Auditorium Filled to Capacity
(more than 4000 seats)
Dr. Ironside Preaching, 1938

adhered without equivocation to all the truths which are pillars of the faith; for example, the verbal inspiration of the Old and New Testament Scriptures, the virgin birth and deity of Christ, the necessity for and efficacy of His atoning sacrifice for sin and the sinner, His bodily resurrection from the grave and His ascension into Heaven, His premillennial return to the earth to judge and rule, that man's salvation is by God's grace through faith, and all that these doctrines involve.

Harry's resonant and powerful speaking voice was a tremendous asset to his preaching. He knew how to use it and had no need of the amplifying facilities so important today to many preachers and singers who would be otherwise ineffectual, not only outdoors but in large auditoriums as well. At the same time HAI's voice was expressive and warm. It could be bathed in pathos or harsh with contempt.

Ironside's popularity as a speaker was further augmented by the unaffectedness of his person, the authority with which he spoke, the evident clarity of his thoughts, the simplicity of his teaching, and the brevity of his talks, which rarely exceeded thirty-five minutes. He felt that if he could not get his message to the audience in that length of time it was not worth preaching, and furthermore, that it was better to say too little than too much.

An exceptionally retentive memory aided HAI immeasurably. Steeped in the Scriptures, as he was, it is not astonishing that he was able to call forth passage after passage of the Bible without having consciously memorized them. Many men who are constantly on the platform are able to bring to their minds instantly cita-

tions they need from the Word. But Harry had virtually total recall of anything he had ever read—not only
from the Bible but from hymns, poems, and secular
literature also. While addressing an audience he might
quote an obscure poem and, when asked about it later,
say it was something he had read thirty or forty years
earlier in his life.

One of the most astounding examples of HAI's
memory took place about a year before his death, at a
time when he was almost completely blind because of
cataracts in both eyes. I heard him give a series of
verse-by-verse studies of the Revelation over a period
of two weeks. Before each message someone read a
chapter of Revelation. Then Dr. Ironside expounded
that chapter, introducing each verse in its proper se-
quence and explaining the meaning of the verse, then
going on to the next verse, and so on through the
chapter, not once having to have his memory refreshed
by the rereading of a particular verse or even a clause.
This is fantastic.

Many speakers have a keen memory of Bible
passages, not because they have made a point of learning them but because of constant reading of the Scriptures. I myself used to cite long passages of the Bible
as I spoke. I could also recite some of the shorter books
or important chapters from beginning to end. But
never, never could I have interrupted myself after each
verse, expound it, and then pick up where I had left off
in the passage. Harry Ironside possessed a remarkable
gift from God which he was able to employ for the glory
of God.

A friend wrote me of having been at a service in
Durham, North Carolina, where Ironside was the speaker.

This was in 1949. An old lady sat down next to her and said, "When my children told me there was a big preacher from Chicago here, I said, 'Well, I ain't goin.'

"They said, 'Aw, Mamma, go once and if you don't like him, don't go any more.'

"Well, I ain't missed a night, and he ain't said a thing I ain't understood."

It was his simplicity that made Harry Ironside profound.

16

OF MAKING MANY BOOKS

Harry Ironside's first commentary on a book of the Bible was published in 1905 by Loizeaux Brothers. Twenty-five years later, when HAI assumed the pastorate of Moody Church, he had written many volumes: thirty-two clothbound books and twelve booklets, a total of forty-four titles. This was only a beginning. From 1930 to 1948, when he resigned as Moody Church's pastor, he turned out thirty-eight additional volumes—twenty-six major books plus a dozen pamphlets. Ironside's final commentary, *The Prophet Isaiah*, was finished only several weeks before his death and was published posthumously in 1952, about which more will be said in due course. Even though some of his one hundred titles,* specifically his expositions of Bible books, were taken down stenographically or on tapes from messages delivered at Moody Church, Ironside was obliged still to edit the manuscripts before they were sent to the publishers.

The distribution of Harry's books is remarkable and is still going on after a quarter century. A fair estimate would be that the total sales of his expository and miscellaneous volumes equals well over a million

*For a complete list of titles by H. A. Ironside, see Appendix A.

copies. In addition, perhaps 750,000 booklets, pamphlets, and tracts have been circulated. Six institutions have published HAI's writings: American Tract Society, William B. Eerdmans, Loizeaux Brothers, Moody Press, Fleming H. Revell, and Zondervan Publishing House.

The relationship between H. A. Ironside and his major publisher, Loizeaux Brothers, who brought out all but fifteen of his writings, lasted for about a half century. It was uniquely personal. Through the years all the Loizeauxs who have been directly connected with the business have been warm friends of HAI, especially P. Daniel Loizeaux, second-generation head. In a desire to perpetuate the purpose of the founders, he relinquished ownership of the firm, which was then reorganized as a nonprofit religious corporation. Both the firm and the author were born the same year, 1876. The Christian witness was contiguous. In 1948 Elie Loizeaux, who had been saved under Dr. Ironside's ministry at the Old Tent Evangel in New York, was the third generation to assume leadership. He invited HAI to send a greeting to the directors at their annual meeting. Dr. Ironside recorded a message, which is cited below in part.

April 9, 1948

I count it a privilege to have this opportunity of sending a word of greeting to the directors of Loizeaux Brothers, Incorporated. As you all know, I have been closely identified with your publishing house for nearly half a century, from the time that you published my first title book, *Notes on the Book of Esther*, right up to the present day. During this time almost fifty volumes have been brought out by you and I certainly appreciate the fine spirit of cooperation and the high Christian standards that have always been maintained by your firm. I pray most earnestly that in these days of business perplexity, when so much is needed in the way of rearrangement, that all needed wisdom will be given in order that you may continue the marvelous ministry that God has given you, of getting out books and pamphlets on Biblical subjects that will be the means of blessing to untold thousands of God's people throughout this and other lands. . .

I wonder if there will not be a wonderful revelation at the judgment seat of Christ when you see the many, many people who have been brought to a saving knowledge of our blessed Lord through your literature. That certainly will be a great reward, a crown of rejoicing in that day. . . .

Just at present I am in Dallas, Texas, where for two weeks I am giving lectures on the book of Revelation to the students of the theological seminary here. . . . A number of these young men will be going out as missionaries to various foreign lands and others will be pastors and evangelists in the homeland and over in Canada. The truths they are learning here and the right things that are embodied in the books you publish will be used by them in passing on the Word to others. I have been particularly pleased to notice how interested many of them are in having such sets as C.H.M.'s *Notes* and J. N. Darby's *Synopsis of the Books of the Bible* and F. W. Grant's series of *The Numerical Bible.* If their hearts and minds are filled with the truth that is embodied in these books there is no telling how God may use them in ministering to others in days to come. . . .

May the Lord bless you, give you a good time together as you wait before Him, and lead and guide in all future planning and arrangements.

H. A. IRONSIDE

Dr. Ironside never accepted royalties for his own use but instructed his publishers to withhold his fees and, upon notification from him, to send gift copies of his books to ministers, missionaries, students, and others whom he might designate. Moreover, in several instances he requested Loizeaux Brothers to contribute from his balance in their hands specified amounts of money to the free literature fund of the Western Book and Tract Company.

In 1942, when Harry was named president of the

Africa Inland Mission,* he sent a form letter to every one of the nearly 300 A.I.M. missionaries on the field, offering to supply them without charge any of his books they might request. When the late Ralph T. Davis, who was at that time general secretary of the mission, saw this letter, he said to Dr. Ironside, "I wish I were on the field so that I might take advantage of this generous proposal." As quick as a wink Harry replied, "Son, thou art ever with me, and all that I have is thine."

There were occasions when Ironside was irked, even hurt, when he realized someone was taking advantage of him. For instance, after a church service he might promise to send a set of books to a student who professed to be rather hard up, only to observe, a few minutes later, the young man driving away in a shiny new car. But such experiences were not many and did not deter HAI from pursuing his established practice. He said he was willing to be misused by a few in order that a multitude might be helped along the way.

Two books that Harry wrote during the Moody Church years deserve special comment. The first is entitled *Except Ye Repent.* In 1936 the American Tract Society offered a prize of $1,000 for the best treatise on one or more essential evangelical doctrines of the Christian faith. The contest was open to all and closed on August 31 of that year. Dr. Ironside thought often of submitting a manuscript but could not seem to get started because of his other duties. Finally, in the last week of July, he began work on *Except Ye Repent*, and from then until he completed the book he wrote in

*For a complete list of organizations with which HAI was affiliated, see Appendix B.

longhand, on trains and at conferences, mailing the chapters as they were finished back to his secretary in Chicago, Miss E. L. Dowe, who typed the pages for him there. He completed the manuscript of some 54,000 words, on the closing day of the contest. His diary reads:

> August 31, 1936
>
> Finished my book on *Except Ye Repent* and had it in the mail at 5 P.M. Mr. and Mrs. Sutherland took me to the station to register it. Will it win the $1,000 prize? I hardly dare even to hope!
>
> November 25, 1936
>
> Was greatly pleased, but somewhat surprised to get a telegram today notifying me that I had won the $1,000 prize in the A. T. S. Book Contest.

The second book is *A Historical Sketch of the Brethren Movement.* Harry's fellowship with the Brethren, as we know, was always a happy one. He realized that in bringing out this volume, which points not only to the merits of Brethrenism, which are many, but also to the sad divisions, he would offend some of them. He hesitated long before having the work published. Would it not be better to eliminate any criticisms? But would that be entirely honorable or fair? He concluded that a frank treatment of the whole movement, as he knew it, would in the end be the best thing, and he prayed that some of the leaders among the Brethren might be as exercised as he himself was, if they were not already, so that some good might come from the publication of the book.

The volume has been widely read and its author strongly criticized. Yet it is an honest expression of HAI's conviction concerning the value and the failures of Brethrenism—that Brethrenism is the nearest approach to New Testament church order possible, lacking apostolic conditions and apostolic power, and is marred only by human weakness. The preparation of *A Historical Sketch of the Brethren Movement* was a labor of love on behalf of those men and women for whom he always had a sincere and respectful affection.

In June 1942 Bob Jones College (now Bob Jones University) conferred upon HAI his second honorary degree, Doctor of Divinity (D.D.). For a number of years Ironside was opposed to receiving what might appear to be praise from men. When in 1930 he accepted an honorary degree from Wheaton College, Illinois, he excused himself on the basis that this degree, Doctor of Letters (Litt. D.), was earned. The citation spoke of it as being in consideration of his contribution to evangelical literature. Now, however, he faced a quandary: should he accept an honor that he had at one time opposed for other people? His explanation of his affirmative decision was that he was grateful to his friend, Dr. Bob Jones,* and did not want to offend him by rejecting the favor.

"Furthermore," he said, "a lot of people thought I was a possessor of a D.D. degree and would advertise me thus. Now I am saved a great deal of explanation."

The late saintly D. M. Stearns once told me, "I know of only one wholly consistent man who ever walked this earth. He was crucified at the age of thirty-three."

*Dr. Bob Jones, Senior, founder and first president of Bob Jones University.

17

LEAVING ONE ANOTHER WE TOOK SHIP

In August 1931 the author of this book, who was at that time publisher and managing editor of *Revelation*, a Bible study magazine, was having luncheon in Philadelphia with two directors of its publishing firm. I asked these two gentlemen about their summer vacations. One of them mentioned a trip he had taken, adding that he would like to have attended a Bible conference but, since he had only three weeks off each year, there was not time to do that and see something of the world too.

"Wouldn't it be nice to do both?" I asked. Then a thought came to me: Why not?

The following week I visited the offices of the Cunard Steamship Company in New York and talked things over with one of their executives. The result was that within a few weeks I chartered, on behalf of *Revelation* magazine, the *S.S. Transylvania*, a 23,000-ton ship, for eight days in July 1932. Ports of call were to be Hamilton, Bermuda, and Halifax, Nova Scotia. The cost of the charter was $65,000, but I had no doubt we could persuade enough Christian people to take this Bible conference cruise to make up a full complement of passengers. *Revelation* was a new magazine which was

On the S. S. *Transylvania*—the *Revelation* Cruise, 1932

Homer A. Hammontree
Paul Beckwith
E. Schuyler English
Reginald Wallis

Will H. Houghton
Donald Grey Barnhouse
Harry A. Ironside
William Allan Dean

built on the name of its editor, Donald Grey Barnhouse, who, as pastor of the historic Tenth Presbyterian Church in Philadelphia, radio preacher, and itinerant Bible teacher, had a very large, enthusiastic following.

To make this unique Bible conference as appealing as possible I knew that we must have some outstanding speakers. Dr. Barnhouse was in France on vacation, and as he was essential for the success of the venture, I cabled him, inviting him to be one of our speakers. Of course he accepted. The next speaker we had to have, I felt, was H. A. Ironside. He, too, accepted the invitation. We filled out the panel with men such as Will H. Houghton, then pastor of the Calvary Baptist Church in New York; Captain Reginald Wallis, secretary of the Y.M.C.A. in Dublin, Ireland; and William Allan Dean, minister of the Aldan Union Church in suburban Philadelphia. Homer A. Hammontree, widely-beloved gospel singer, was engaged to lead the music with the help of his accompanist, Paul Beckwith.

So it was that HAI, together with Edmund and Freda Ironside and their little daughter Marion, left the North American continent for the first time on July 14, 1932 for a journey that was short in time and distance. Harry enjoyed it immensely, as excerpts from his diary revealed.

July 14, 1932

Warm in New York, but ideal sailing weather. Left the Cunard pier on the *S.S. Transylvania* at 12 noon and had a wonderful cruise all afternoon and evening. First meetings of the series on A deck at 8:30 and 10 P.M. Barnhouse, English, and Wallis spoke. Many friends on board.

July 15, 1932

Good night voyage and fine A.M. meeting. Brumbaugh and Wallis speakers. Ed, Freda, and baby having a good time.

In the afternoon I gave an address on "Christ in Galatians."

At night Dr. Houghton and W. A. Dean spoke on different helpful themes. Have had a wonderful day.

July 19, 1932

Reached Halifax early. About 800 people were waiting on the wharf to welcome us. Brother Turner met me and took our family party for a drive. At 3 P.M. we had a meeting on the wharf—1,000 present. Barnhouse spoke and I followed on Romans 1:16-17. Left at 4 P.M.

The meeting on the pier, to which HAI refers, was one of the great experiences of my almost half century of Christian commitment. About 1,000 men and women stood on a cement floor in a huge storage shed drinking in every word. They sang hymns together as Homer Hammontree led them from a podium that was, in reality, a 15-foot-high platform used in directing the loading of freight. Acoustics were abominable. However, both Barnhouse and Ironside had powerful speaking voices and were heard clearly by everyone despite the absence of a microphone and amplifiers. When the *Transylvania* sailed away there were tears in the eyes of many on the ship's deck and on the shore.

July 20, 1932

The weather was perfect and the sea calm all day. The meetings were good. We closed at 10:30 P.M. with a Communion Service, some 500 participating.

Tomorrow our wonderful cruise comes to an end, much to our regret.

July 21, 1932

The glorious cruise ended when we docked in New York at 2 P.M. Ed and family left for Boston, and I visited Loizeaux Brothers ere leaving. Got my mail and attended to a few matters of importance.

Mrs. Theodore Keller of New Canaan, Connecticut, was among the passengers on the *Revelation* Cruise. Several years later at a Bible conference on the grounds of the Stony Brook School on Long Island, New York, where Dr. Ironside was one of the speakers, Mrs. Keller observed how tired HAI was and learned that, except for his voyage on the *Transylvania*, he had not had a vacation in nearly forty years. This bothered her. Two weeks later, when Harry was back in Chicago, he received a surprise.

> August 26, 1935
>
> I received today an offer from Mrs. Keller to pay all expenses for Mamma and myself for a ten weeks' tour to Palestine next fall or spring. Am looking to God for guidance.

After he and "Mamma" talked it over they decided that this was a provision from the Almighty for a needed rest for Harry and that, in addition, a visit to the Holy Land would be helpful in his ministry. Would it not be wonderful if they could take Lillian with them, they thought. She would lose a year of school, but the year would be profitably spent and there was no special need for her to graduate with her present class. The trip would enlarge her whole life. Consequently, as they began to plan the trip they began to save for Lillian's fare. Furthermore, HAI did not know when he might have another opportunity to cross the Atlantic Ocean. So they made arrangements to return from abroad by way of England and Scotland, for Harry longed to visit the land of his forefathers. So that he could do this, Moody Church granted him a full three months' leave of absence.

On February 4, 1936 the three Ironsides boarded the *S.S. Exochorda*, a freighter whose eventual destination was Beirut, Syria. There were not many people with whom Harry and his family were congenial, and there was considerable drinking among a few of the passengers. However, after a few days the Ironside party found some who were eager for Christian fellowship, among them several Baptist missionaries.

The first Sunday Harry was asked to lead a deckside church service, which opened a way later for him to speak to a number of people, both passengers and crew. He reported that "most are without faith and care nothing for eternal things." After the ship put in at Gibraltar for a few hours to unload freight, she went on and docked at Marseilles on Sunday. Harry wished he knew of some place of worship, but since he did not, he walked the streets of the city for several hours distributing French tracts.

At length the *Exochorda* landed at Beirut. The Ironsides disembarked and traveled by motor to Baalbek and Damascus before turning toward Jerusalem. In Damascus they walked along "the street which is called Straight" and saw the place where the Apostle Paul is reputed to have been let down over the city wall in a basket (see Acts 9:11,25).

On then to what HAI had been looking forward to for so long—Jerusalem. En route the party passed through Capernaum and viewed the ruins of a synagogue there which may well have been the one that a certain Roman centurion built for the Jews (Luke 7:5). Harry was reasonably sure that this was the very place; so he stood for a few moments on the rostrum where the Lord Jesus may have taught nineteen centuries earlier (Mark 1:21).

The three travelers' first sight of Jerusalem was shortly after noon on February 28. They rested for a while and then the party went sightseeing. In the morning they walked with Hyman Jacobs, a Hebrew Christian who acted as their guide, through David Street to the Wailing Wall where, HAI writes, "we bowed our heads and prayed for the redemption of

Israel. A great crowd was there reciting the peniten-
tial Psalms." The afternoon was spent motoring to
Jericho, the Jordan River, and the Dead Sea. The next
day was Sunday. Let the diary speak.

March 1, 1936

Lord's day in Jerusalem! What thoughts crowd in upon us!
We broke bread with an assembly of "brethren" at 10 A.M.

At 2 we went out to see Calvary (Gordon's) from the wall of
Jerusalem near the Damascus Gate—then to the Garden
Tomb.

At 3:30 I preached in the Baptist Chapel on "The Sinless
One Made Sin." 70 present.

At 7:30 I preached in the American Church—200 present,
on "The Mission of the Holy Spirit," John 16.

It has been a memorable day. . . . Enjoying fellowship so
much with many Christians here.

Three days later the Ironsides left Jerusalem* After
spending almost a week in Cairo they sailed for Naples
and went on to Rome, where they had a marvelous experience seeing innumerable historic sights, including,
of course, the ancient Coliseum and the Mamertine
Prison, where St. Paul was held in chains before he was
beheaded by Nero.

London was the next stop of special consequence to

*What moved HAI most in Israel, I think, was his visit to the Garden Tomb.
The Church of the Holy Sepulcher, in the center of modern Jerusalem, is
reputed to be the site of Christ's burial and of His resurrection. It is shown
to the vast majority of tourists in the Holy Land as one of the Biblical land-
marks. The Garden Tomb, on the other hand, is not a popular tourist at-
traction. It is, by the way, privately owned by the Church of England.

The garden is at the foot of Gordon's Calvary, which is the most likely site
of Christ's crucifixion, known as the Place of the Skull. The tomb is a rock-
hewn cave on the side of a hill, quite evidently a new burial place in Jesus'
time. Only one slab in the tomb is completed, which has a place at its head
like a stone pillow. The opening of the tomb is low, so that a person of
average height must stoop to enter. See Matthew 27:60; John 19:40-42; 20:3-
8. One of my most treasured memories is of a visit to the Garden Tomb on
Easter morning many years ago. The garden is enclosed now within walls
and is a lovely restful spot. The tomb has a cleft high above the entryway
and, as the sun rose on that Easter morning, its rays shone brightly on the
pillow of stone.

Harry. They reached the city on March 21.

> March 21, 1936
>
> At last another dream of my life has come true. We are in London, the great world-metropolis, and it does not seem greatly unlike New York or Chicago.
>
> We left Paris about noon, going to Calais, thence across the Channel to Dover, and then by train to London. The Channel, of which we had often heard disquieting reports, was calm as an inland lake.
>
> My cousins, Mabel and Ernest Neale, met us; also McAdams. In two cars they brought us and our luggage to the Kingsley Hotel. . . . They took us for a drive to see the great city by night. We enjoyed it all and praise God for His goodness.

During the next thirty days the Ironsides visited in England, Scotland, and Ireland: London, Edinburgh, Aberdeen, Glasgow, Kilmarnock, Belfast, Bangor, and Dublin. In many ways it was not unlike the days in America, for HAI spoke thirty-one times to audiences ranging from around 200 to 1,200. In London they followed the program of most tourists, but Dr. Ironside also visited places and institutions of which he had heard and with which he had corresponded in years past—Pickering and Inglis; Marshall, Morgan, and Scott, publishers of *The Life of Faith;* and others.

One of the high points of the travelers' tour of the British Isles was a visit to Aberdeen, the country where the Ironsides had their roots. The last Saxon king of England was Edmund Ironside. He was murdered by Canute but his two sons escaped and carried on the family name. A prominent personage at the beginning of World War II who, after his retirement, spent time researching the history of the Ironside family, was General Sir Edmund Ironside. Harry had some correspondence with Sir Edmund a few years after his visit to Aberdeen.

One memorable day HAI looked upon his father's old home.

> April 6, 1936
>
> This was to me a most interesting day. We drove over to New Deer and Cairnbano—the district from which my forefathers came. Saw the house where my own father was born—the place at Cairns or Southfield where the family lived, etc.
>
> Preached at night in the Assembly Hall before large audience. I took up "Perfect Love." Good interest, and I hope some were blessed.

Soon thereafter the party of three returned to the United States, Harry feeling physically and mentally refreshed.

Three other trips to England followed in successive years. The Moody Bible Institute commemorated its centenary in 1937. Special meetings were held all across the United States and Canada, and for several months in England also. The late Will H. Houghton, then president of the Institute, arranged for an exchange of speakers between Britain and Scotland, bringing Bishop J. Taylor Smith and Evangelist Jock Troup to America and sending Dr. Ironside and Evangelist Mel Trotter to England. Harry was there for thirty-two days, speaking sixty-two times. Ten thousand people were present for the opening service in Royal Albert Hall, London, where Lord Aberdeen presided. Harry spoke on that occasion on Romans 1:16. Other meetings were held in London at Central Hall, Westminster, and the Aldersgate Y.M.C.A. In Edinburgh the two Americans preached in famed St. Giles Cathedral.

When he got back to Chicago a number of invitations came to HAI as a result of his ministry in the British Isles. So in 1938 a party of six sailed to Ireland—Harry,

Helen, and Lillian Ironside, Stratton and Marjorie Shufelt, and Mrs. Eunice Hay, a member of Moody Church. This was to be an evangelistic tour. It opened at Templemore Hall, Belfast, and moved over to Glasgow, where meetings were held in Tent Hall and the Play House. Audiences ranged from 300 to 4,500, except on inclement evenings. A number of men and women responded to the gospel of Christ night after night. Other campaigns were carried on in Kilmarnock and Aberdeen.

The tour ended with a ten-day series in Kingsway Hall, London, with about 2,000 persons in attendance. The party returned home glorifying God for evidences of salvation of souls through the preached Word, and by the gospel as it was presented in song by Shufelt, whose ministry was appreciated everywhere.

Ironside visited Britain again in 1939. He had been invited to give the Bible messages at English Keswick in July and planned to cross over alone just for the week's ministry, but in April the Laidlaws arrived in Chicago from New Zealand with their two sons, John and Lincoln, and daughter Lillian. Harry had not seen his sister, Lillian, in eight years; in fact it was only the second time in almost twenty years that Bert and Lillian had been in America. Bert suggested that Harry ask for leave of absence from Moody Church so that he could go abroad with them in May for a motor trip throughout Great Britain before Harry needed to meet his appointment at Keswick. Harry did not need much persuasion, for he was quite worn out from the schedule he had been carrying. So the five Laidlaws and HAI sailed from New York on the *Queen Mary* on May 24. For the next fifty days Harry had virtually a complete rest, speaking only eighteen times as the group toured England, Wales, and Scotland.

Back home in Chicago once again, Ironside resumed his church responsibilities and his self-chosen, demanding outside program. What may have been his crowning work during the Moody Church years, that is, beyond the church ministry, was a campaign that he undertook in Oakland, California, in the winter of 1944. With Stratton Shufelt as his musical director and soloist, HAI, assisted by his son, John,* went "home" for an evangelistic effort of eighteen days. Thirty churches in Oakland united in sponsoring these meetings which were designed specially for defense workers and service personnel. As the campaign progressed the audiences in the Oakland Civic Auditorium grew larger night by night until the place was filled to capacity in the closing days.

Many people came to a saving knowledge of Christ. The effort took its toll of HAI, as his diary indicates:

---

*The last previous mention of John Schofield Ironside was concerning his return to Oakland in 1931 from a round-the-world cruise on one of the Dollar Steamship Company's "President" ships, on which he served as a purser. In 1927, his senior year at the University of California (Berkeley), John, who as a lad had been a bright Christian, slipped into a spiritual eclipse, experiencing many and varied doubts about the Scriptures and spiritual matters generally. In 1932, while he was with the Dollar Line, John married Miss Sally Gentry. Several years later he went into business for himself for a short period and then, in 1939, he was graciously restored to the Lord. John and Sally gave themselves completely to Christ and together entered the Moody Bible Institute, from which they were graduated in 1941. Subsequently John served as associate pastor of Moody Church until 1944, dean of men of the Moody Bible Institute until early 1947, manager of the Winona Lake Bible Conference in 1947-1948, and finally pastor of College Baptist Church, Manhattan, Kansas, until his death of a heart attack in January 1957 at the age of fifty-one. John Ironside's widow, Sally Ironside, currently (1976) lives in Indianapolis, Indiana. Her daughter, Martha Bernice Ironside, lives in Dayton, Ohio, where she has a position.

February 25, 1944

. . . left me very weary mentally.

However, God, who delights to use weak things, came in at night. Some 2,100 present. I preached on 2 Corinthians 5:21. Many stood to confess Christ and about forty came forward to be dealt with. It rejoiced our hearts to see this break.

With this we conclude the review of Harry Ironside's public ministry, which began in 1890 when he was a boy preacher and continued for sixty years, until his death in 1951. It was a distinguished testimony for Christ, "not . . . in word only, but also in power, and in the Holy Ghost, and in much assurance."

18

A MAN AFTER GOD'S OWN HEART

The life story of Harry Ironside cannot be punctuated with his inner thoughts and general
philosophy. It is a tale of a man in motion. He had little
time for the kind of meditative essays that may be
found in the writings of the Puritans and the saintly
authors of the nineteenth century. This is not to say
that Harry did not commune with God. How could a
man live in the Scriptures as he did without honoring
and adoring the Persons of the Godhead—God the
Father, God the Son, and God the Holy Spirit? He
delighted in knowing by his own experience the favor
of God, a fact that is easily discernible in his diaries.

Today has tried me much but "I will trust, and not be
afraid." . . . Thou knowest, O Lord.

My 38th birthday. Surely more than half my life is done.*
Even though the Saviour's coming should not take place in
my time, it would seem to be very near. Oh, to use the time
that remains more for God than the time that is past.

Cares weigh my spirit, and I find it difficult to rise above
them. Lord, help me to confide in Thee more implicitly.

"Reckon ye yourselves dead indeed unto sin" (Romans
6:11). I feel very keenly how feebly I enter into all this.

*A fair prophecy! The date of this diary entry is October 14, 1914. HAI
went to be with Christ on January 15, 1951 at the age of seventy-four years
and three months.

Harry was devoted to his family, and while the relationship between him and Helen was not always smooth, this is not astonishing. It is not that Helen was unsympathetic with his calling or not proud of his accomplishments. However, Harry's zeal for Christ and conscientiousness in exercising it took him away from home so much—sometimes for weeks or months—that life was not easy for his wife. This may be somewhat of an understatement. The responsibility of bringing up and disciplining two young boys was entirely hers. Furthermore, for more than twenty years the household was run on a hand-to-mouth financial program. This disturbed Helen. It is easy to cite an old adage that "all is well when it is God's hand that feeds our mouths," a maxim that is true indeed; but ask anyone who has lived "by faith" how difficult His testing is sometimes. Helen trusted the Lord to supply her needs according to His promises, yet making ends meet required that she stretch the cord mighty tight sometimes.

Helen was somewhat temperamental and it bothered her that so many silly women made a fuss over her husband. When he was home she was possessive of him; when he was away from home she was jealous of him. There can be no question that Harry had a burning compulsion to preach the Word whenever and wherever he could do so and rarely declined an invitation to speak, unless it was physically impossible for him to accept. But there *is* some question as to the wisdom of his extended absences from his home. It is not fair to Helen, however, to suggest that she opposed Harry's itinerant ministry. Often in their early days they prayed together about the matter. The Lord came first in their lives—this was always so. They sought

His will and submitted to it insofar as they knew it. Many commercial salesmen are on the road as much as Harry was, and Harry was an ambassador of the King! Should he sacrifice less than they?

In the thousands of pages of HAI's diary he mentions again and again his affection for Helen. He reveals that he missed her a great deal, that he was thinking of her and remembering such-and-such an occasion and how much he disliked being away from his family. No matter what city he visited he tried to find some little gift to take to her when he should get home. It might be only a piece of ribbon, a handkerchief, a small trinket of some kind, but almost always something. I know this because I was with him on a number of occasions when he did his shopping—often at a drugstore or a five-and-ten, to be sure, but this only because he had little money to spend. In later years he was able to do better. For example, one time Harry brought a present from Canada. His diary reads: "Helen was delighted with some English china I brought over." On another occasion, when HAI had been in Dallas for the week preceding Good Friday and Easter, he came home without a gift. The next night he wrote in his journal, "After lunch I went down town [in Chicago] and bought a couple of dresses for Helen. She likes them very much." There is pathos in Harry's comments in his 1947 journal, when Helen was quite ill. After having completed a series of messages in Florida he wrote:

> March 4, 1947
> En route to Chicago. Was thoroughly tired physically and mentally, and slept nearly all day. . . . I keep thinking of Helen and hoping and praying all is going well with her.

Here and there comments appear about "poor Helen" this and "poor Helen" that, or "Helen sick at 11

P.M. Had to be up with her all night," or "Helen cough-
ed a great deal," and "Helen is not at all well. I am
much concerned about her." Only about one entry in
nearly 7,500 pages suggests less than complete accord
between husband and wife, and this was at a time when
she was unwell.

June 30, 1947
> Helen does not seem well. She broods a good deal. I wish
> there might be more of the joy of the Lord.

With Harry Ironside there was never anyone else
than Helen Schofield Ironside. She was the wife of his
youth and of his mature years also. It would never have
occurred to him to look at another woman. Once, when
a lovely lady chided him gently for not recalling that he
had met her several years earlier at a certain Bible conference, he responded, "Well, you know, I simply don't
remember all the nice ladies I meet. You see, I have a
perfectly good wife at home."

During their half century of marriage the Ironsides
experienced times of rejoicing and times of sorrow.
Their two sons, both of whom wandered far from the
Lord as young men, were restored to Him. It will be
recalled that Edmund came back to Christ after he and
Freda had lost all that they possessed in the Florida
hurricane of 1928. The senior Ironsides were filled with
joy at Ed's return to the Lord, and then in 1939, when
John and Sally committed themselves to Christ, Harry
wrote:

> The thing that has meant more to us this month than
> anything else has been a letter from John telling of his sur-
> render to Christ for full-time service. It was so wonderfully
> written, and is the answer to our prayers of many years—
> and it just broke us down before the Lord.

In the summer of 1941 HAI was scheduled to direct
the General Conference at Montrose, Pennsylvania.

During the train trip from Chicago he was quite concerned about Edmund, who had suffered a coronary thrombosis a few days earlier. Harry's journal on the day of his arrival reads:

> July 25, 1941
>
> Reached Buffalo at about 8:45 and left on D. L. & W. at 10 A.M. Arrived at New Milford about 4:50 and was driven to Montrose.
>
> Just after dinner I received a telegram from Freda telling me that Edmund had just passed away. I have a son in Heaven—but oh, how I shall miss him down here!

I was with Dr. Ironside that day, since I too was to speak at the conference. Understandably Ed's death at forty-two was a great shock to his father, who seemed stunned. After communicating with Helen and John he made arrangements to leave the next day for Dallas, where he preached Edmund's funeral sermon. The topic: "Thanks be unto God for His unspeakable gift." Entries in the diary are too personal and too sacred to be cited.

More than two hundred friends, both black and white, attended the service. No higher compliment to Ed and to his understanding of and interest in the black students at the Southern Bible Training Institute could have been paid than that which was spoken by one of them, "Edmund Ironside was the blackest white man I ever knew."

Life and work must go on, and within a few days HAI was back in the harvest field. Yet the shock of Edmund's death weighed heavily upon him for many months and left him brain-weary. He knew that the Lord does all things well. He rejoiced for Ed, but try as he would he seemed unable to cast off a blanket of grief. Time heals, though, and in due course—really through the months of sorrow—Harry's confidence in the love of God and His peace sustained him. Writing me later about Edmund and his seemingly unfinished task, HAI said:

> Nature would try to raise questions, but faith rests in the sense of the infinite wisdom and love of God. Our hearts find wonderful peace as we dwell on the blessed estate of the dead in Christ. Surely nothing can be more wonderful than this: "They shall see His face." And then when we talk of work interrupted, we need to remember there is a work over yonder doubtless far more important than anything which can be done here, for it is written: "His servants shall serve Him."

In 1934 Harry purchased a house in Wheaton, Illinois, because Lillian was to enter Wheaton Academy that autumn. He had seen the faith of his sons wrecked in secular institutions of higher learning and he wanted to spare Lillian that travail. It seemed senseless for her to commute between Chicago and Wheaton and, in view of the fact that he himself was away from the city much of the time during the week, the Wheaton house could serve as home for Helen and Lillian. On weekends they could come into Chicago, where he would still maintain an apartment in the Plaza Hotel.

Lillian graduated from Wheaton Academy in 1938 and from Wheaton College in 1943. In 1944 she married Gilbert Koppin, Jr. who was in the armed services at the time, receiving his discharge in 1946.* In 1944, therefore, Helen moved back to the hotel in Chicago.

Throughout his whole life Harry had little time for relaxation, especially after the mid-twenties. In the California years he went fishing several times but, as he admitted, he caught very few fish. "Others got some

---

*Currently (1976) the Koppins live in Indianapolis, Indiana. They have three sons—Gordon, John, and David.

Edmund H. Ironside
1936

John Schofield Ironside
1941

Left: Lillian Ironside
(Mrs. Gilbert A. Koppin) 1943

Below:
Harry and Helen Ironside
on their Fifteenth Anniversary
at Moody Church, 1945

fine trout," he wrote once, "but I do not seem to be an expert." Ironside was fond of music too. He would occasionally go out to Idora Park in Oakland and listen to an outdoor band. One of the entries in his diary reads:

May 17, 1913

Very tired and weary physically and mentally today, so after lunch went to Idora Park and sat quietly in the open air and listened to a band, which I enjoyed and found quieting and soothing.

Philately was Harry's special hobby. He had unusual opportunities to gather stamps in his Moody Church years, for not only did the church support more than one hundred foreign missionaries but in addition he, as president of the Africa Inland Mission, was in personal correspondence with hundreds of other servants of Christ in Africa. Ironside was never timid about asking people for special stamps because in return he would promise to send them some of his books. Time and strength to enjoy fully this hobby were wanting. Only infrequently does his journal mention spending an evening sorting stamps.

Harry never really learned to play. The fact is that he never wanted to play. His one great passion was to make Christ known by preaching the gospel and expounding the Scriptures. How could he idle away the time, he thought, when there was so much to be done? His thoughts ran to the world's greatest need and all else was sublimated to that. "Lord, save the lost!" "Would that Christ were more before these people!" "O God, revive Thy work in the midst of the years!" These thoughts ruled his mind. It was most difficult for him, even as a young man, to sit still while needy men and women were on their way to a Christless grave. His attitude may be summed up in a journal entry made way back in 1914. He and Helen had gone to the home of friends for dinner and, upon his return to their own house, he wrote:

> July 16, 1914
>
> A great feast they had in Spanish style. . . . Music and dancing followed, and I could only sit in a corner and I fear I was considered rude and peculiar. Ah, well—my day is coming. Then I, too, shall dance!

Do not suppose that Harry Ironside never erred. In his peak years he was held in high esteem by almost all evangelicals. He was often spoken of facetiously as the Archbishop of Fundamentalism, a title that amused him but also, I suspect, pleased him. There were occasions, however—not many of them—when he toppled from his high pedestal in the esteem of several of his intimates and other admirers—when he allowed bitterness to rule over his normally impartial judgment. I have no doubt that in every instance HAI was confident of his rectitude. When all is said and done, his heart was open before God. It was his life's pattern to seek the Lord's will and to do it. He knew of some of his own imperfections and that there were other failings of which he might be unaware. Harry, like King David (who certainly was not without faults), was a man after God's own heart, whose greatest desire at all times was to be right with the Lord.

I knew HAI quite well for about thirty years and spent many hours with him, not only at Bible conferences and committee meetings but also visiting the sick upon occasion and in fellowship with other believers. I found him headstrong sometimes, but agreeably so and usually willing to grant other people benefit of doubt. When I told his daughter-in-law, Sally Ironside, that I thought it would be foolish to pretend in this book that HAI was perfect, she replied, "I know you're right, but it's hard for me to realize he was anything but perfect." This, mind you, of one who was her father-in-law for nineteen years!

Ironside possessed a keen sense of humor. He was not a person to tell jokes just for a joke's sake, but he had a way of seeing the amusing side of incidents of daily living and would draw on them. "I think I know what Paul's thorn in the flesh was," he said once, "it's his choir director."

Many times in his early travels Harry was provided with accommodations that were anything but comfortable, to say the least. There were occasions when he was obliged to share a room or even a bed with a boy or young man of the household. No complaint can be found in his journals except by inference, such as when he wrote: "I have a bed all to myself! As I am a real crank about sleeping alone I know I shall enjoy it." Over all, however, Ironside felt that his friends treated him far better than he deserved. I recall the first time I arranged for his accommodation was in Philadelphia in 1933. I had reserved a room for him in the Drake Hotel, which was considerably better than what he was accustomed to. Coming down to the lobby to meet me for dinner, he said, "My dear brother, you have engaged far too luxurious accommodations for me."

Fearing that he might think he would have to pay the bill, I assured him that it was already taken care of.

"Yes, I know," he said, "but I should hate to have the Apostle Paul see me coming out of this place. This is hardly learning to be abased!"

"Perhaps you have already learned that," was my answer.

"Oh, well," he replied, "Paul said, too, that we should learn to abound. But you shouldn't do this for an old tramp like me."

When I was preparing to write an earlier biography of HAI, he wrote to me:

January 6, 1943

My dear Brother:

When you get to doing my biography, please be careful to get facts. Recently it has been stated in print that I am rather a big fellow, for two inches has been added to my stature, something the Lord Himself intimated could not be done.

On his sixty-eighth birthday he took time to send a handwritten note:

October 14, 1944

Beloved Brother:

I do not feel appreciably older today, although I suppose I should—but that will come later on. You remember the story of the Scot who celebrated his one hundredth birthday. A friend said to him, "Well, Sandy, I congratulate you, but I'm afraid ye'll no be here to celebrate a second hundred." To this Sandy replied, "I'm not so sure of that. The fact is, I am feeling very much stronger to begin this second hundred than I was when I began the first."

Never one to ask money for himself, Harry had a genuine interest in a number of evangelical enterprises and it gave him pleasure to tell the Christian public about them. As a consequence he was frequently asked at Bible conferences to "lift the offering," and he never declined these opportunities, so much so that he said that, should the Lord not come again before his death, he was sure the engraving on his tombstone would read:

AND THE BEGGAR DIED ALSO

The impression of HAI that was left with those who knew him well was of his unfailing thoughtfulness and kindness. For example, he was punctual. I suppose I must have called for him in various places forty or more times. Never did he keep me waiting but was always at the appointed place at the appointed time.

Another illustration of his thoughtfulness comes to mind in relationship with his associates at Moody Church, for whom he did many things. When Herbert J. Pugmire joined the pastoral staff in 1947, he and his family moved into an apartment in Oak Park, Illinois.* Herbert is a large man and mentioned to HAI that he never seemed able to find a comfortable chair. A week or so later Harry asked him to go shopping with him and, while they were in a furniture store, HAI looked at some stuffed upholstered chairs and said to his associate, "Herbert, try that chair and see if it's comfortable." The younger man thought his pastor was looking for something for himself, but he sat down in the chair anyhow.

"Is it comfortable?" Harry asked.

"Yes, it is."

"Are you certain?" Ironside inquired; and when Pugmire assured him that it was, Ironside ordered the chair, telling the salesman to deliver it to the Pugmire address, but to send the bill to H. A. Ironside.

Another evidence of HAI's kindness was his custom of listening to every message of every speaker who shared in a conference program with him, no matter how young or inexperienced or even boring that person might be. Not many well-known preachers are so thoughtful. Furthermore, Ironside would always try to say a word of encouragement to these people, if it was

*Currently (1976) Dr. Pugmire is president of the Heritage Baptist Institute, Cleveland, Ohio.

At Bible Conference, Stony Brook, Long Island, New York, 1936
Henry Woll, E. Schuyler English, Isaac Page, H. A. Ironside,
Miss Frances E. Bennett, Homer A. Hammontree, Wilbur M. Smith,
Paul Beckwith, Wm. C. Thomas

The Directors of Winona Lake Bible Conference, c. 1942
Back Row: E. D. Given, Amos Neuhauser, Elmer B. Funk, George W. Cooke
Middle Row: Bob Jones, Jr., Charles M. Woods,
Gaylord A. Barclay, McElwee Ross, Harry A. Ironside,
Samuel M. Morris, Henry Hepburn, Peter J. Zondervan,
F. Russell Purdy, B. H. Gaddis, Harold Strathearn.
Front Row: Fred Strombeck, H. Earl Eavey, J. Palmer Muntz,
Mrs. William A. Sunday, R. G. LeTourneau, J. A. Huffman,
Homer A. Rodeheaver, Arthur W. McKee.

Speakers at English Keswick, 1939

Back Row: R. A. Laidlaw, E. L. Langston, W. Wilson Cash, Colin C. Kerr

Middle Row: W. D. Jackson, W. B. Sloan, T. M. Bamber, A. Lindsay Glegg, Montague Goodman, A. W. Bradley, Guy H. King

Front Row: Francis Outram, Lionel B. Fletcher, J. M. Waite (Hon. Treasurer), W. H. Aldis (Chairman of Trustees), Harry A. Ironside, W. W. Martin, C. H. M. Foster (Hon. Secretary), J. R. S. Wilson.

The Author
H. A. Ironside
and Homer A.
Hammontree
at Montrose,
Pennsylvania
1948

possible to do so. Sometimes it was not possible. Then he confined his remarks to his diary, as for example, "I heard Dr. — — — last night . . . a wretched case of misapplication of Scripture."

Not from Harry Ironside but from some who have benefited from his benevolence I have learned of dozens of incidents which reveal unusual grace on the part of a busy man. I mention just a few. A poor, young preacher came to see HAI in his office—discouraged, with no church and no engagements. After talking with him Harry sent him through the Moody Bible Institute, starting him on his way with a new suit of clothes. . . . Calling upon a long-time friend in a distant city, HAI discovered his friend was not at home and talked with his now-grown daughter. He asked her if she had received Christ as her Saviour and, upon hearing a rather uncertain reply, said to her, "You know, dear girl, I hope you will trust in Him. I have prayed for you many years, and I shall continue to do so." . . . A Pullman porter with whom HAI chatted on an over-night journey, to whom he sent a set of expository books. . . . A friend with whom Harry had lunch artless-ly mentioned that his financial circumstances might require him to withdraw his daughter from college. The next day the man received a check from Ironside for ten dollars with a promise of a like amount every month until the young lady should graduate.

I shall never forget a personal experience of some quarter century ago. Ironside was speaking for a week at a young people's Bible conference situated about eighteen miles from our summer cottage. I drove down there at noon one day to bring him back to our home for lunch. I mentioned, when we shook hands, that it was my wife's birthday. When he learned this he walked over to a bed of flowers on the conference grounds and, stooping down, picked a few and got into the car. Mrs. English said that the picture she would carry of him to her dying day was of his getting out of the car when we reached our cottage and walking down the driveway with the little bouquet in his hand. Nothing could have made her happier than this act of thoughtfulness on the part of a busy and weary man. It was something that anyone might have done—but few other than HAI would have done it.

19

THE SANDS OF TIME

When Harry Ironside became pastor of the Moody Church in 1930, the church's indebtedness amounted to $319,500, a large sum of money in those days. On December 31, 1943 the final note of the indebtedness was burned. The benevolent outreach of the church was not curtailed so as to accomplish this; in fact, whereas there were ninety-two Moody Church missionaries on the field when HAI assumed the pastorate, one hundred and seven were being supported when the mortgage was discharged.

By 1944 Ironside, who had assumed personal responsibility for notes totaling about $15,000 owed by the Western Book and Tract Company, repaid all the investors who desired reimbursement and reorganized the firm into a nonprofit religious corporation.

The year 1946 was Harry's seventieth. He began to think about resigning his pastorate, feeling that he was now too old to appeal to young people. Furthermore, he was obviously aware that his audiences were beginning to diminish. For the past year the Sunday morning worship services attracted only about 2,500 people, which means that while the first floor of the auditorium was usually full, the gallery was sparsely occupied. One of the reasons for this, of course, was the city's gradual migration to the suburbs. To commute to the church was inconvenient, especially in inclement weather, and it was fairly expensive. Two trips a day were most difficult for many of the members. Ironside felt that a younger and more dynamic man than he might be better for the church. As he sought the Lord's will he continued his usual grueling schedule.

A marked change took place in the lives of the Ironsides in 1947. Helen's physical condition, resulting from a coronary thrombosis, was worsening—not pain, actually, but weakness and severe headaches kept her miserable. Entries in HAI's annual journal read like this: "Helen worse." "Helen had a very bad night." "Sat up with Helen part of the night." "Thought Helen was slipping away." At the same time Harry's vision was failing. Both his eyes, in which cataracts had begun to form several years previously, were becoming more and more cloudy, although the cataracts were not sufficiently formed to require surgery, or so he had been told. He was able to keep on with his work, although with some difficulty. Only the day after he wrote to a friend, saying, "My sight seems to be leaving me," his diary notation reads:

> Worked in the office till noon. "Ezekiel" now ready to be mailed. Thank God. It is probably the last large book I shall ever be able to write.*

In September, while he was in Memphis for a series of meetings, he called upon Dr. Wesley McKinney, a Christian friend and distinguished eye surgeon, who

---

*HAI was mistaken. His volume, *The Prophet Isaiah,* was finished late in 1950 and published posthumously in 1952. See comments about this book on page 226.

advised an operation whenever HAI could arrange a convenient time.

The journals were now written in a scrawl that became increasingly difficult to decipher. Just discernible is a comment made on November 24, 1948: "I realize that I am a tired old man." On December 31 about 1,800 people attended the Watch Night Service at Moody Church. The next day Harry wrote in his diary:

> During the past year I have given 569 addresses besides participating in many other ways.
>
> As the year closes my dear wife Helen is still in a very serious condition, but we are hoping that it may please God to raise her up and spare her to us for some time to come.
>
> John [Ironside] left us today for Winona Lake after having been with us four days, as we both felt that the worst was over and that we might expect Helen to improve from now on.

This statement has been copied from the last page of the last diary Harry Ironside ever kept. From this time on he owned a diary but used it only to make notations concerning dates and places of future speaking engagements.

January 5, 1948 marked the Ironsides' Golden Wedding Anniversary. The occasion was celebrated at the church but it lacked luster because the "bridegroom" was there without his "bride." The ceremony was piped over to the Ironside apartment at the Plaza Hotel so that Helen, who was there with her now constant companion Miss Anna,* could hear the toasts and comments and Harry's responses to them. She was pleased with everything.

Mrs. Ironside's periods of discomfort increased as

---

*Miss Anna was a competent and compatible registered nurse.

the months passed. Only seldom was she despondent; most of the time she enjoyed the pleasures that were available to her. She did not lose her interest in life; for example, she was very fond of animals and used to watch the horses and carts she could see from her hotel window. She felt the optimism that her physician and family had expressed to her at the turn of the year, and she had the added pleasure of Harry's presence a great deal more than in years past, for he now accepted few out-of-town engagements—only in places within twenty-four hours' reach of Chicago.

Sometime in mid-1947 HAI had made an engagement to speak for several days in Minneapolis in April 1948. As the date approached he felt reluctant to leave Helen. He told her he thought he should cancel his appointment, but she urged him to carry on, reasoning that God had called him to preach the Word, she was no worse than she had been for several weeks, and there was really nothing he could do for her at home. They prayed about the matter and with common consent he departed. A few days later, while Harry was on the train returning from Minneapolis, Helen was taken into the presence of the Lord. The time was 2 A.M., May 1, 1948. Gilbert and Lillian Koppin, with Miss Anna, met the train at the station in Chicago and broke the news to HAI.

The funeral service was held at the church. Associate Pastors Hermansen* and Pugmire respectively opened and closed the service; Beverly Shea, gospel soloist, sang two of Helen's favorite hymns,

---

*Howard A. Hermansen, who went to Moody Church upon HAI's invitation shortly after World War II, is currently (1976) retired and living with his wife in Shell Point Village, Fort Myers, Florida.

"Great Is Thy Faithfulness" and "I Shall Be Satisfied";
Dr. J. Palmer Muntz of Winona Lake spoke a few ap-
propriate words; Dr. Henry Hepburn, once pastor of
the Buena Memorial Presbyterian Church, read the
Scripture; and Dr. William Culbertson, president of the
Moody Bible Institute, preached the funeral sermon.
Helen's body was buried in the plot Harry had purchas-
ed only months earlier.

Harry blamed himself because of his absence when
Helen died. For months he seemed to carry a sense of
guilt which he could not be persuaded was unnecessary. It was nothing more than the emotional
reaction of an aging and tired man.

Not many weeks after the Lord took Helen, Harry
had a misadventure, doubtless due to his failing sight.
He fell down a flight of stairs at the church and against
a door leading out to La Salle Street. Pugmire and
others who heard the noise rushed down to help him.
They found him sprawled on the floor stunned, and
they lifted him up. He complained that his shoulder
hurt him but insisted it was really nothing. He would
go over to the apartment, he said, and put some lina-
ment on it. Pugmire told HAI that he would do
nothing of the sort, that he (Pugmire) was going to
drive him to the hospital for an X ray. Harry
protested—no hospital for him, he said; he had
engagements to keep. But Herb Pugmire was adamant
and almost carried him to the car for the drive to the
Swedish Covenant Hospital in Chicago. The X ray
revealed that HAI had a broken shoulder.

The Pugmires insisted that Ironside stay in their
apartment in Oak Park for a while rather than that he
should be at the Plaza Hotel alone. The Koppins lived

in the same apartment building as the Pugmires, so Lillian would be able to attend to some of his needs. Meanwhile the Pugmires would stay elsewhere. Arrangements were made and carried out, and for several weeks HAI spent his days reading and working while seated in the comfortable chair he had given Herbert Pugmire the preceding year. The preacher of Ecclesiastes said, "Cast thy bread upon the waters: for thou shalt find it after many days" (11:1). So Harry's kindness to his associate returned to him in Oak Park.

On May 30, 1948 Pastor Ironside submitted his resignation to the executive committee of the Moody Church, to become effective October 31. The resignation was accepted "with exceedingly great and heartfelt regret," and with thanks to God as expressed below:

> . . . for these eighteen fruitful years, during which he has been so mightily used here, and elsewhere throughout the country, and abroad, in the salvation of hundreds, yes, thousands of precious souls, in the building up of the saints in their most holy faith, and in the example of Christian meekness and humility he has demonstrated. . . . It is our fervent prayer that, as the Lord tarries, He may continue to use this talented and consecrated instrument of His grace, in the labor he so loves, the sowing of the seed, the cultivating of the vineyard, and the harvesting of the souls of men and women for whom Christ died.

As much as Harry loved the church and the sheep over which God had made him shepherd, now that his decision had been made and his resignation submitted and accepted, he could hardly wait for the next four months to pass. He still experienced periods of depression about the fact that he was not with Helen when God took her, and he missed her. Sometimes, when he was coming home late after a speaking engagement, he automatically stopped in an Italian fruit store near the

Plaza to buy a tidbit to take up to Helen, as had been his custom—until he was brought to a halt quickly, remembering she was not there. To a prominent member of the church's executive committee he confessed one day that he felt his work on earth was accomplished, that the sands of time were sinking rapidly, and he was waiting eagerly to be taken to Heaven.

From Wednesday, October 27, through Sunday, October 31, farewell meetings arranged by various organizations of the church were held to honor their beloved retiring pastor. They were happy occasions, of course, although it seemed to some of the people as though the ministry of Moody Church could hardly go on without Dr. Ironside as leader and guide. That was shallow thinking and not worthy of them. God has a servant prepared for every task and, knowing this, their despair was short-lived. HAI's final remarks may be summed up in these words:

> My heart's desire and prayer to God for all of you is that through grace each may be led into a deeper knowledge of Christ and a more intense love for the Word of God. Let me close with the words of the Apostle Paul to the elders of Ephesus, "I commend you to God and to the word of His grace, which is able to build you up and to give you an inheritance among all them that are sanctified." I shall look forward with joy to the great reunion at the coming of our Lord Jesus Christ and our gathering together unto Him. How good it is to know that Christians never meet for the last time!

So ended HAI's Moody Church years. God's servant, who sixty years earlier as a lad of twelve prayed, while he was listening to D. L. Moody preach, "Lord, help me someday to preach to crowds like these, and to lead souls to Christ," had finished his course at the church that Moody founded.

PART 5

OLD AND FULL OF YEARS

"Well done, good and faithful servant:
thou hast been faithful over a few things,
I will make thee ruler over many things;
enter thou into the joy of thy lord."

MATTHEW 25:21

"For we preach not ourselves, but Christ Jesus the Lord;
and ourselves your servants for Jesus' sake. For God,
who commanded the light to shine out of darkness,
hath shined in our hearts, to give the light of the
knowledge of the glory of God
in the face of Jesus Christ.
But we have this treasure in earthen vessels, that
the excellency of the power may be of God, and not of us."

2 CORINTHIANS 4:5-7

20

ALL THIS AND HEAVEN TOO

After Harry resigned from the pastorate he moved down to Winona Lake, Indiana, where he began living with the John Ironsides. This was to be his headquarters, although he was there only rarely; for relieved of Moody Church responsibilities he was now able to engage again in an itinerant ministry even though he was dreadfully handicapped because of the cataracts in his eyes. He could read only with greatest difficulty, this requiring that he hold printed matter close to his face. Had he not been saturated with Scripture and blessed with a fantastic memory he could not have pursued his distinctive expository preaching.

In January 1949 HAI fulfilled a long-standing engagement at the Central Presbyterian Church in St. Petersburg, Florida, where he taught the Bible for two weeks. He was lodged on the second floor of the church in an apartment known as "the prophet's chamber." It had a refrigerator and an electric stove, so that Harry could get his breakfasts there, but it was better to go out for other meals. Various people, including the pastor and his wife, Dr. and Mrs. Edward R. Barnard, entertained him sometimes, either in their homes or in one of the many hotels and restaurants in St. Petersburg.

Two widowed sisters from Georgia—Mrs. William Harrison Hightower of Thomaston and Mrs. W. Roy Finch of Macon, had attended Central's winter Bible conference for several years, and this particular season they made it a point to come down to St. Petersburg during the period that Harry Ironside was scheduled to speak. So it came about that they became Harry's guides and chauffeurs, while they took him on pleasant drives and to attractive eating places.

Ann Hightower had met Harry a few years earlier, but the occasion was not much more than an introduction after a church service. During the St. Petersburg conference, however, she and Harry struck up a warm friendship. He was drawn to her first by her kindness, and in ensuing days by her charm and wit. To his great loss he was unable to see clearly her lovely face. Ann Hightower was attracted to Harry first by his mastery of the Scriptures and dynamic presentation of the Word of God, and then by his mind and his humility, warmth, and guilelessness—also, I suspect, because she felt he needed her. At any rate, after HAI returned to Chicago he happened to meet the man whom he had told a few months earlier about his readiness to be taken to Heaven. He confessed to his friend, "You know, I met a lovely lady while I was in Florida, and I find myself not quite as eager to go to Heaven right now as I was when I spoke to you last."

In the weeks that followed Ironside had several appointments in the southeast and, whenever he did and she was able, Ann Hightower managed to be visiting somewhere in the area of his ministry. It was not very long before these two dear people were betrothed. The marriage was planned to take place sometime in the

Ann (Mrs. W. H.) Hightower
and Harry Ironside
at Winona Lake, Indiana
in the Spring of 1949

Robert and Lillian (Watson) Laidlaw
at their Home in Auckland, New Zealand
January 1971

Harry and Ann Ironside on Their Wedding Trip
at the Author's Summer Cottage in Pennsylvania, October 1949

autumn, a fact which of course set some tongues wagging. Cruel gossip. Harry was then seventy-two years old, almost blind, and rather helpless. Ann was about twelve years younger than he, loved him, and was eager and able to serve him in many ways. Why should they wait around for a fitting time? What time could be more appropriate than right then? She lived in a gracious southern home in Thomaston, Georgia. Her family was quite agreeable to the marriage,* and HAI's children approved it wholeheartedly.

On October 9, 1949 Henry Allan Ironside and Annie Turner Hightower were married by Dr. Graham Gilmer, pastor of a Presbyterian church in Lynchburg, Virginia, where HAI had just concluded a series of meetings.

The newly-married couple's wedding trip was surely not one in the usual sense but certainly fitting, with the joyous tempo that their lives together were to have. From Lynchburg they went up to Hagerstown, Maryland, and the next day came to our summer cottage in Skytop, Pennsylvania, for an overnight visit. From there they went to Toronto, Ontario, where Ann took Harry's dictation—a lesson for *The Sunday School Times*. This was the first secretarial chore of many tasks she would perform in the months that followed. From Toronto, where Ann met "dozens of Harry's cousins," the Ironsides continued their itinerant service for Christ in Washington, D.C.; Durham, North Carolina; Augusta, Georgia; and so on for months. In a number of church services, because

*Mrs. Hightower had three living children, all with families of their own: William Harrison Hightower, Jr. and George Harrison Hightower of Thomaston, and Martha (Mrs. Harry J.) Davis, who was at that time living in Germany but currently (1976) in Washington, D.C.

HAI was unable to see to read the Bible when he began his message, Ann read the Scripture portion for him. She did it beautifully and captivated audiences with her well-modulated voice and soft Georgia accent.

Back in Thomaston for Christmas and the early part of the year, Harry began champing at the bit to return to the gospel trail, even though he found Ann's southern home restful and its leisurely life different from anything he had ever known. Elie Loizeaux, of the publishing firm, wrote HAI, asking him if perhaps Mrs. Ironside would be willing to read the galley proofs of Harry's book on Joshua.* Harry's reply throws light on what a godsend Ann was to him:

January 21, 1950

My dear Brother:

My "charming lady" says she will be delighted to read the galley proof on Joshua. "Reading proof is one of the fondest things she is of." She is really an expert at it. I can't tell you, Elie, what joy she has brought into my life and of what assistance she has been to me. You would hardly believe it but we have traveled by automobile over 9000 miles since we were married October 9 and she has borne up wonderfully under all the strain of driving and looking after a half-blind man, so that I could only thank God from the depths of my heart for giving me such a partner in the work.

H.A. IRONSIDE

Ironside had been writing lessons for *The Sunday School Times* for about fifteen years. He enjoyed the work, finding it a blessing to his own soul as he compared Scripture with Scripture while drawing his thoughts together to prepare the weekly manuscripts. It was necessary that the lessons be written months before their publication in the *Times* and early in 1950

*Composed of lectures delivered some time before this and edited for the purpose of publishing them in a single volume. For a complete list of titles by H. A. Ironside see Appendix A .

he came to the conclusion that he would have to relinquish this phase of his ministry. On June thirtieth, therefore, he wrote to the late Philip E. Howard, Jr., editor of the *Times*,* stating that he was on that very day, just before leaving Thomaston with Mrs. Ironside for a speaking tour, mailing the lesson for the last Sunday of 1950. After expressing his regret that this was the termination of that particular task in the Lord's work, he said:

> For the last six months it has become increasingly difficult for me to do this [write the lessons] owing to my nearly blind condition. If it had not been for the help of my dear wife in reading to me and looking up the references and then writing out the lesson in longhand to my dictation, I do not know how I could have gotten through. This is what I mean when I say I lay down this work with a feeling of relief.
>
> I want to thank you personally for your kindness and consideration throughout these years, and assure you that it has been a real joy to work with you in this way.

There began at this time a set of providentially-arranged circumstances that were to effect the completion of H. A. Ironside's final book-length commentary. During World War II there was a young man in the United States Navy named Ray C. Stedman who, among his other wartime duties, was ordered to serve as a naval court recorder. Stedman read several of HAI's expositions, which had been recommended to him by a friend and, when the war ended, Ray and his wife, Elaine, went to the Dallas Theological Seminary in preparation for the ministry. When they reached Dallas in the autumn of 1946, Stedman was overjoyed to learn that Dr. Ironside was one of the annual visiting lecturers at the seminary. After hearing Harry for two

*Dr. Howard went to be with the Lord on Christmas day, 1963, after a long illness following surgery for a brain tumor.

weeks there, the young man was so impressed that he devised a way to get to know this great Bible teacher better—Ray suggested to HAI that he be permitted to take his dictation whenever Ironside was in Dallas and help him in any other way that he could. He offered to do this for nothing. Anyone who knew HAI well would have known that he would never accept such an offer from a young student, and indeed he did not do so on this occasion. The two came to an agreement: Stedman would take his "pay" in Ironside books.

In 1950 Harry lectured at the seminary for two weeks on the book of Isaiah and Stedman took the talks down on a wire recording device. He did not have sufficient wire to record the whole series, so he had to wipe off the early chapters, and use that same wire for recording the later chapters, beginning at chapter 40.

When these Dallas lectures were finished, Dr. and Mrs. Ironside proposed to Ray that, upon his graduation from seminary in the spring, he should accompany HAI during the summer months as a combination chauffeur and secretary. During that period Elaine Stedman and the children could visit with her family at Great Falls, Montana, where Ray would join them in time to begin a ministry in Palo Alto, California, to which he had been called. Mrs. Ironside, even though it was her chief joy to be with her husband and serve him in every way possible, was too wearied physically to continue his demanding traveling schedule without respite. Ray could relieve her so that she might spend some time in Thomaston, and she could join them occasionally when it was convenient.

Ray accepted the proposition and everything went off beautifully. Dr. Ironside and Ray worked on HAI's book on Isaiah. Stedman would read a portion of a chapter aloud and then read from commentaries by F. C. Jennings and W. E. Vine. Harry would remain silent for a few minutes while he arranged his thoughts, after which he would dictate his exposition of that section.

"I was always amazed," Stedman wrote, "at the way he kept his comments from being simply a 'rehash' of Vine and Jennings, but always managed to bring out some interesting sidelight which the others had overlooked."

By the time the chauffeur-secretary association was brought to a close, Harry had finished the first thirty-five chapters of the book.

For Ray Stedman this experience with Dr. Ironside was one he will never forget. HAI's love of the Scriptures, his eagerness to preach the whole counsel of God, and the simplicity of his messages, which were addressed to the heart rather than to the intellect, had a tremendous impact on Ray's life and ministry. Upon leaving Harry and Miss Annie (as Ray called Mrs. Ironside) in August at Binghamton, New York, Ray went to Montana for a short rest and then took his family to Palo Alto, where for a quarter century he has carried on a vital, unique, and ever-enlarging testimony for Christ at the Peninsula Bible Fellowship.

In September 1950 Dr. McKinney removed HAI's cataracts. The operations, performed three days apart, took place in Memphis. Ann and her sister, Mary Finch, stayed at a hotel in the city to be near Harry, and John Ironside came down from Winona Lake. The surgery was successful and a week later Harry and Ann went back to Thomaston. For several weeks Harry used temporary lenses in his spectacles; then on

October twenty-fifth he and Ann picked up the permanent lenses in Memphis. As Ann expressed it later, he "could see perfectly for six beautiful, happy days."

Harry had been promising the Laidlaws for many years that someday he would visit New Zealand. He and Ann were to sail from Vancouver soon to fulfill that promise and, from New Zealand to proceed around the world for meetings planned in various places, concluding with the Keswick conferences in Ireland and Britain. En route from Memphis to Vancouver by train they had a stopover of several hours in Chicago. This happened to fall on a Sunday morning, so the Ironsides decided to go up to Moody Church and attend at least part of the morning service. Before it started they visited with a few friends and, when it was time to begin, Carl Armerding, a gifted and greatly-beloved Bible expositor who was to preach there that day, invited HAI to share the platform with him and to read the Bible at the appropriate time. Ironside read with facility; in fact, Ann told me later, "He was so delighted to be able to see that he was showing off a little."

It was then time for the Ironsides to leave for their train connection. Dr. Armerding came down from the pulpit with HAI and escorted both of them to the door. Returning to the pulpit he passed Mrs. Armerding, who was seated in the front row of the auditorium, and leaning down whispered to her, "We'll never see Harry again on this earth."*

Indeed HAI was "delighted to be able to see." Within the next few days he sent postcards to several

---

*Lillian Ironside Koppin, HAI's daughter, used almost the same words to herself when, in Atlanta in the early summer the Ironsides put her on a plane for Indianapolis: "I'll never see Poppa again in this life."

of his friends, his comments written in such miniscule letters that, when I read mine, I was reminded of the people who say they can write the so-called Lord's Prayer on the head of a pin.

A series of meetings was scheduled in Vancouver before the Ironsides should sail for New Zealand. Here at their hotel what seemed a tragedy occurred. Harry slipped in the bathtub and, in falling, struck his right eye on a faucet. The physician in Vancouver did not want Harry to sail and Ann also thought they should postpone the trip. But HAI insisted he was going and at length the doctor gave him permission to do so provided he would remain quietly in his bunk for a stated number of days. During the voyage Harry stayed quite still until they were about to dock at Honolulu, where he left the ship for a drive in the countryside and enjoyed a visit on shipboard with several friends. When they put to sea again HAI taught the Bible on several occasions in the ship's lounge.

New Zealand at last! The Ironsides stayed with the Laidlaws in their beautiful home in Auckland, overlooking the harbor. It was a happy visit. Lillian Laidlaw had longed for years that her brother might come, and a quarter century after the visit still cherishes the short time they had together there. Her devotion to Harry is expressed in a letter written to Marie Loizeaux* in February 1975:

> To me Harry was more than a brother, for my mother went to Heaven when I was five and my father when I was sixteen, and while I had dear, kind guardians my brother was very "special" as a wonderful example of Christlikeness and all that I admired most. His thoughtfulness to me as a child growing up was wonderful.

*Miss Marie D. Loizeaux, editor at Loizeaux Brothers, Inc.

On shipboard and also after they arrived in new Zealand Harry, with Ann as his secretary, completed chapters 36—39 of his commentary on Isaiah. But how was the book to be finished? You will recall that Stedman, when he sat under Ironside while HAI taught the book of Isaiah at Dallas Theological Seminary, did not have sufficient wire to record the whole book, and therefore had to wipe off the early lectures, beginning his recording with chapter 40, and finishing with the last of Isaiah's prophecy, chapter 66. This wire was transferred to discs which, after Harry's death, were sent to Loizeaux Brothers to complete the commentary. It was not wholly incidental that at the very next chapter after HAI ceased his writing of the commentary, Ray Stedman's recordings were ready for use. This was the hand of God.

During the month between the Ironsides' arrival and Christmas Harry spoke several times, in one instance to an audience of about 3,000 in Auckland's Town Hall. After Christmas the Laidlaws and the Ironsides spent a week in Taupo, where the Laidlaws owned a lakeside cottage. There Harry completed his very last expository writing, a commentary on Revelation 6:1-6 for *Our Hope* magazine. It was mailed to me on January 9, 1951. Then on to Rotorua, where HAI was to speak on Sunday, January fourteenth.

In the morning, when the Ironsides were about to leave the hotel for the meeting hall, Harry told Ann that he was not well; it was probably, he thought, a touch of indigestion such as he had supposed he had had while in Taupo—at least a doctor there had diagnosed it as such. Actually, it was a heart attack. Nevertheless, Harry took part in the meeting. His

Scripture was Psalm 118:19-29, beginning with the sentence, "Open to me the gates of righteousness: I will go into them, and I will praise the LORD." His voice did not sound like his own. After the service Bert Laidlaw insisted that Harry consult a physician, who told him he must go immediately to the hospital. "No," Harry said, "I'm scheduled to speak this evening." However, he was taken to the hospital at 5 P.M.

Following the evening service, where Bert Laidlaw substituted for Harry, Ann and the Laidlaws went to see Harry at the hospital. When they entered his room, Ann asked him, "Darling, shall we read our usual chapter together?"

"I have just read seven chapters," was his answer.

The three visitors stayed only a short time and then left, with assurances that they would see him in the morning. At 3:30 A.M. they received a telephone call notifying them that Harry Ironside had gone Home. The date, January 15, 1951.

Ann thought that Harry's funeral service should be held at Moody Church. There were certain complications, however, and after a telephone conversation with John Ironside in the States, it was agreed that it would be best to lay HAI's body to rest in New Zealand, in Purewa Cemetery. Bert Laidlaw conducted the funeral service at Howe Street Chapel in Auckland.

Years ago I suggested as an epitaph for HAI, should he be taken before the Lord comes, Robert Wild's *Epitaph* "for a godly man's tomb," written three centuries ago:

HERE LIES A PIECE OF CHRIST; A STAR IN DUST;
A VEIN OF GOLD; A CHINA DISH THAT
MUST BE USED IN HEAVEN ,
WHERE GOD SHALL FEAST THE JUST.

Instead, a modest bronze marker at Purewa reads:

HARRY ALLAN
IRONSIDE
14th OCTOBER, 1876
15th JANUARY, 1951
FOREVER WITH THE LORD

POSTSCRIPT

For a number of years Dr. Ironside had a close friend, Alex H. Stewart, a Brethren expositor of Racine, Wisconsin. As early as the nineteen thirties they made a covenant between themselves that, should the Lord not come in their lifetime, the survivor of the two would preach the other's funeral sermon. A. H. Stewart was still living on January 15, 1951 but could not fulfill the agreement because Harry's body was buried in New Zealand.

On February 4, 1951 a memorial service for H. A. Ironside was held in the Moody Church in Chicago. Mr. Stewart kept the covenant he had made with Harry as best he could under the circumstance. Dr. Carl Armerding shared in paying tribute to their old friend, citing the influence HAI had had on his ministry. Dr. Ralph T. Davis, head of the Africa Inland Mission, read the Scripture. Elie Loizeaux, as HAI's publisher, spoke of his lovely character and humility as an author, and of the privilege it was to make his books available to others. Homer Hammontree and Howard Hermansen sang a duet, "The Crowning Day Is Coming." All the living members of the immediate Ironside family were present.

In August 1951 W. Douglas Roe, executive secretary of the Montrose Bible Conference Association, arranged for a memorial service to be held in the conference auditorium. Thelma Porrit and George Edstrom, old favorites of HAI, sang and this author gave the address. The text was 2 Corinthians 11:26-28, "In Journeyings Often."

ACKNOWLEDGMENTS

Much of the information concerning the major portion of Harry Ironside's life story, from the date of his birth until 1944, was drawn from my earlier biography entitled

H. A. IRONSIDE
Ordained of the Lord

published in 1945. For what follows until HAI's Home-call in 1951 I am indebted to:

the Ironside family: HAI's widow, Ann Hightower Ironside; his sister, Lillian (Mrs. Robert A.) Laidlaw of New Zealand; his daughter, Lillian (Mrs. Gilbert C.) Koppin; a daughter-in-law, Sally (Mrs. John S.) Ironside; and a granddaughter, Marion (Mrs. Allen I.) Crawford;

two former associate pastors of Moody Church, Howard A. Hermansen and Herbert J. Pugmire;

the present (1976) pastor of Moody Church, Warren W. Wiersbe, and Dr. Wiersbe's secretary, Linda Beth Ford;

HAI's friend and one-time secretary-chauffeur, Ray C. Stedman;

Herbert A. Fryling, executive secretary of the American Scripture Gift Mission, who was formerly associated with *The Sunday School Times;*

and Elie and Marie Loizeaux, members of the publishing firm for their cooperation and courtesies shown in many ways.

I am also greatly obligated to Ruth Hill English, my wife, for many helpful suggestions and to my long-time friend and former secretary, Joan B. (Mrs. William R.) Hazelton, for typing the manuscript of this book as an act of love.

To all of these dear people I express here my deep gratitude.

E. S. E.

APPENDIX A

A COMPLETE LIST OF TITLES
BY H. A. IRONSIDE

All of these writings were published by Loizeaux Brothers, Inc. unless denoted otherwise.

EXPOSITORY VOLUMES

Joshua, Addresses on the Book of
Ezra, Notes on the Book of
Nehemiah, Notes on the Book of
Esther, Notes on the Book of
Psalms, Studies in Book One of, chapters 1—41
Proverbs, Notes on the Book of
Song of Solomon, Addresses on the
Isaiah, Expository Notes on the Prophet
Jeremiah, the Weeping Prophet; Notes on the
    Prophecy and Lamentations of
Ezekiel the Prophet, Expository Notes on
Daniel the Prophet, Lectures on
The Minor Prophets
Matthew, Expository Notes on the Gospel of
Mark, Expository Notes on the Gospel of
Luke, Addresses on the Gospel of
John, Addresses on the Gospel of
Acts, Lectures on the Book of the
Romans, Lectures on
Corinthians, The First Epistle to the
Corinthians, The Second Epistle to
Galatians, Messages on
In the Heavenlies (Ephesians)
Philippians, Notes on
Colossians, Lectures on
Thessalonians, Addresses on the First and Second Epistles to the
Timothy, Addresses on the First and Second Epistles to
Titus, Lectures on the Epistle to (*See also Hebrews*)
Philemon, A Brief Exposition of the Epistle to

Hebrews, Studies in, with Lectures on Titus
James, Expository Notes on the Epistle of
Peter, Expository Notes on the Epistles of
John, Addresses on the Epistles of
Jude, An Exposition of the Epistle of
Revelation, Lectures on the

MISCELLANEOUS VOLUMES

Brethren Movement, A Historical Sketch of the (Zondervan Publishing House)
Care for God's Fruit Trees
Charge That to My Account, and Other Gospel Papers (Moody Bible Institute)
The Continual Burnt Offering, Daily Bible Meditations
The Daily Sacrifice, Daily Meditations on the Word of God
Divine Priorities (Fleming H. Revell Co.)
Except Ye Repent (American Tract Society)
Four Golden Hours
The Four Hundred Silent Years
Full Assurance (Moody Bible Institute)
Holiness: the False and the True
Illustrations of Bible Truth (Moody Bible Institute)
The Lamp of Prophecy (Zondervan Publishing House)
Miscellaneous Papers (*not contained elsewhere*)
  Mission of the Holy Spirit, The
  Praying in the Holy Spirit
The Mysteries of God
Mystery in Daniel's Prophecy: Messages on the Interval between the 69th and 70th weeks; formerly, The Great Parenthesis (Zondervan Publishing House)
Random Reminiscences
Sailing with Paul
Things Seen and Heard in Bible Lands
The Unchanging Christ (Wm. B. Eerdmans/Loizeaux Brothers)
The Way of Peace (American Tract Society)
What's the Answer? 362 Bible Questions Answered (Zondervan Publishing House)
Dr. Ironside's Bible: Notes and Quotes from the Margins, Introduction by Herbert J. Pugmire

BOOKLETS AND PAMPHLETS

Adders' Eggs and Spiders' Webs (Moody Bible Institute/Loizeaux
    Brothers)
After Death, What?
Apostolic Faith Missions and So-called Second Pentecost
Baptism: What Saith the Scriptures?
Bearing About in the Body the Dying of the Lord Jesus
"Billy" Sunday Funeral
The Christian and His Money
Death and Afterwards
Divine Healing: Is It in the Atonement?
The Eternal Security of the Believer
The Holy Trinity
Implications of the Resurrection
Letters to a Roman Catholic Priest
Lectures on the Levitical Offerings
Little Jackie, A Memoir of A. J. Estabrook
Looking Backward Over a Third of a Century of Prophetic Ful-
    filment
The Mass vs. The Lord's Supper
The Midnight Cry
The Mormon's Mistake, or, What Is the Gospel?
No Room in the Inn
Not Wrath, but Rapture, or, Will the Church Participate in the
    Great Tribulation?
The Only Begotten Son (Moody Press/Loizeaux Brothers)
The Oxford Group Movement
The Poems and Hymns of H. A. Ironside (Zondervan Publishing
    House)
The Real Saint Patrick
Removing Mountains
Salvation and Reward
The Stone that Will Fall from Heaven
The Teaching of the So-called Plymouth Brethren: Is It Scriptural?
The Unity School of Christianity
What Mean Ye By This Service?
What Think Ye of Christ?
Who Will Be Saved in the Coming Period of Judgment?
Wrongly Dividing the Word of Truth—Ultra-Dispensationalism
    Examined in the Light of Holy Scripture

TRACTS

Another Gospel
The Blackness of Darkness Forever
The Dying Gambler
For Your Sakes
A Good Sinner
A Hebrew's Search for the Blood of Atonement
How an Actress Was Saved
I'm In for a Good Time
My Conversion to God
The Only Two Religions
The Right Priest for a Death Bed
Too Bad for Heaven and Too Good for Hell
The Tramp Who Became a Deacon
Which Thief?

APPENDIX B

LIST OF ORGANIZATIONS WITH WHICH
H. A. IRONSIDE WAS AFFILIATED
AT ONE TIME OR ANOTHER

Africa Inland Mission—President
American Association for Jewish Evangelism
    Chairman, Advisory Board
American Scripture Gift Mission
    Member, Board of Reference
William Jennings Bryan College
    Member, Board of Directors
Central American Mission—Member, Board of Directors
Christ for America—Member, Board of Reference
Dallas Theological Seminary—Member, Board of Regents
Bob Jones University—Member, Board of Directors
Montrose Bible Conference Association
    Director and Member, Board of Directors
Moody Bible Institute—Member, Board of Directors
Overseas Missionary Fellowship (formerly China Inland
    Mission)—Member; North American Council
Southern Bible Training School
    Chairman, Board of Directors
Western Book and Tract Company—President
Wheaton College (Illinois)—Member, Board of Directors
Winona Lake Bible Conference
    Member, Board of Directors

APPENDIX C
BOOKS THAT HAVE HELPED ME*
by H. A. Ironside

From my early days I have been an omnivorous reader. I am afraid I have wasted a lot of time reading some books that were of very little profit, but in an effort to get a general idea of literature, embracing history, science, poetry, philosophy, *belles-lettres*, and worthwhile fiction, as well as that which was of far more importance than the rest—a knowledge of the Bible and related subjects—I have read as widely perhaps as one so busily engaged as I, could do. But as I look back over the years there are certain books which stand out in my memory and thoughts as having meant more to me than the general run, whether secular or religious.

I think, as a youth, my first appreciation of history was due to reading a series of books seldom seen now and which many would look upon as rather juvenile, namely, the Biographical Histories by John and Jacob Abbott. It was these books that made historical characters live before my mind's eye, and all that I have read since along that line has never blotted out the memory of the thrills that used to come to me as I pondered over these books by the two Abbotts.

I have always had a love for poetry, both secular and religious, but Tennyson and Shakespeare stand out above all others in the secular field, and the *Hymns of TerSteegen, Suso, and Others*, as translated by Mrs. Bevan, have had the greatest appeal to me of any religious poetry.

As to fiction, which I have read somewhat more sparingly than along other lines, I have always felt I owe a great debt to Dickens, whose vivid portrayals of various phases of life

*At some time around the mid-1940's Harry Ironside wrote this article for an evangelical publication. I have been unable to discover where it appeared, but at the time he wrote it he sent a copy to Loizeaux Brothers.

inculcated in my mind a deep appreciation of human values. I turned to Dickens again and again when I attempted to read some modern bestseller and found myself so disgusted with its filth that I consigned it to oblivion. Dickens never wrote a line that he need to have been ashamed of.

I do not speak here of works of science and philosophy, as I do not recall any of these books or set of books that stands out above others as having been of special value to me.

When it comes to expository works, I have no hesitancy in saying that I owe more to five writers of the so-called Plymouth Brethren school than to any one else. C.H.M.'s *Notes on the Pentateuch*, together with six volumes of his *Miscellaneous Writings*,* proved of inestimable value when as a young preacher I was seeking a firm foundation for my faith and a better grasp of Bible truth. Then a little later some unknown friend, to whom I shall be forever indebted, presented me with a set of J. N. Darby's *Synopsis of the Books of the Bible*. I remember well that I literally devoured these five volumes, giving almost every spare moment to them, so that I read them in two weeks' time. I think I am safe in saying that they opened up the Scriptures in their comprehensiveness in a way that nothing else has ever touched. Needless to say, I have familiarized myself with practically everything J. N. Darby wrote and I regard him as far in advance of any of the other commentators on the Bible.

The works of William Kelly, particularly as set forth in his *Lectures Introductory to the Pentateuch, Early Historical Books, Minor Prophets, The Four Gospels, Paul's Epistles, The Acts, Catholic Epistles and the Revelation*, added much to that which J. N. Darby had already opened up to me. These early books of Kelly whetted my appetite so that I

---

*C.H.M. is the abbreviation of C. H. Mackintosh. It is interesting that the very year this biography is scheduled for publication (1976), Loizeaux Brothers is issuing all six of his volumes, *Miscellaneous Writings*, in one volume under the title, *The Mackintosh Treasury*.

was not satisfied until I had read everything else of his, amounting to thirty or more volumes. I admit they are sometimes rather dry and I like to have a glass of water by my side as I read them, but they are clear and definite, and so far as scholarship is concerned, Kelly towers far above many who are held in honor as outstanding theologians and expositors.

When it comes to theology itself, I owe more to the works of F. W. Grant, I think, than even to Mr. Darby and Mr. Kelly. F.W., as he is familiarly known, led me into an appreciation of what I might call the "inwardness" of the great truths of the Person of Christ and His propitiatory work, such as I have never found anywhere else.

Samuel Ridout, who was a close collaborator with F. W. Grant, helped me much, particularly as to setting the example of simplicity in unfolding the truth of God, so that the ordinary mind could readily grasp it.

The following books I have found most helpful in giving me a deeper knowledge of Bible history and connected subjects: Edersheim's *History of Israel and Judah* and also his *Life and Times of Jesus, the Messiah.* Though not absolutely clear as to certain great truths concerning the Person and work of our Lord, both Geikie and Farrar, in their books, both entitled *The Life of Christ*, helped fix certain outstanding facts in my memory that have always been helpful in my study of the Gospels.

Sir Robert Anderson's various books have been a joy and delight because of their keen analysis of great Biblical themes, though unfortunately Sir Robert was during his later years evidently somewhat under the influence of that great scholar, but distressingly ultradispensational teacher, E. W. Bullinger.

I should probably mention in closing that I have been greatly indebted to both Strong and Young in the study of words and their inner meaning. Their great concordances are always within reach and I find them invaluable.

INDEX